WILD MONEY

A FINANCIAL FIELD GUIDE AND JOURNAL

LUNA JAFFE

Fortunity Press

Fortunity Press
7837 SW Capitol Hwy, Suite C
Portland, OR 97219

Fortunity Press books are available for special discounts for bulk purchases. Special editions, including personalized covers and books with corporate logos can be created in large quantities for special needs. For information contact sales at 503-452-7000 or info@fortunitypress.com

Illustrations by Rachel Dominguez-Benner and Rebecca Owens
Book Design by Deandra Ellerbe
Cover Design by Rachel Dominguez-Benner, Hilary Costello and Deandra Ellerbe
Page 11 artwork by Cynthia Morris

Library of Congress Cataloging-in-Publication Data

Jaffe, Luna, date.

Wild Money Financial Field Guide and Journal

 p. cm.

Includes bibliographical references and index.

ISBN 978-1-63620-148-4

1. Personal Finance, 2. Creativity, 3. Personal Growth I. Title.

Printed in the United States of America

10 9 8 7 6 5 4 3 2

First Edition

Contents

CHAPTER 6: Protect Your Potential

CHAPTER 7: Give with Guts

CHAPTER 8: Take Your Wild with You

Zelda's Financial Field Guide

Zelda's Financial Toolbox

About the Author

Index

Your way begins at the other side.
Become the sky.
Take an axe to the prison wall.
Escape.
Walk out like someone suddenly born into color.
Do it now.

—Rumi

Introduction

In your hands is a tool for transformation, a guide book, an ally, a mirror of who you are and who you can become. This is a companion to *Wild Money: A Creative Journey to Financial Wisdom* and these books are meant to be used together. Here you will not only find all the exercises in the first book, but also included are checklists, vocabulary lists and the amazing *ZGuide to Money,* which is a visual glossary of financial terms. You have a process and a tool box for taking the journey so that you can claim your rightful delightful inspirational relationship with money.

You know what my fear is? That you will pick this journal up, fill out a few pages, and then stop dead in your tracks. Life has a way of throwing distractions when we decide to explore the secrets and taboos we carry about money. Even with the best intentions, most people won't complete this process on their own.

So what's the solution?

Circles.

Create a circle and work through the exercises together. Hold each other account-able with compassion and understanding. These circles can be made up of friends in the neighborhood, or virtual friends from around the world. What I know is that this work becomes more powerful and more possible when done in a circle.

I hope you will stay in touch. If you hit a road block, email Zelda@lunajaffe.com, and we'll provide assistance, resources and encouragement. But most importantly, do the work and make it fun. You're worth it and the world needs you!

Wildly Yours,

Luna

HOW TO USE

Prepare

Coloring Pages

Drawing Pages

SCHEDULE IT IN

Find your calendar. . . we'll wait. Block out 15-20 minutes 3-5 days a week, or a chunk of 1-2 hours this week and for the next 7 weeks. Do it now, and make it non-negotiable. You'll be happy you did.

MAKE SPACE

Brew your favorite tea, collect your books + tools, turn off your phone/computer, prepare a cozy place away from distractions. Give yourself the time and space to fully engage in your Wild Money Journey.

BE KIND to YOURSELF

Amidst the break-throughs and a-ha's, you'll likely be traveling through some raw spots. Do your best to treat yourself with compassion and acceptance.

ALLOW PLAY

Each chapter starts with a beautiful black and white drawing related to the theme. Coloring in this page can be a great entrance meditation for the week's work ahead, or a welcome respite if you hit a particularly rough exercise.

MAKE IT YOURS

You'll also find Zelda being helpful throughout your journal. Make these images your own by coloring them in however you like. Get messy, be precise, loosen up, color with your non-dominant hand, or try to make one ugly on purpose. This is your book, have fun!

LOOSEN UP

Even if you tell yourself you "can't draw," dare to draw – it's a powerful change agent. Collage, painting, or Google image searches are also great tools for getting your image down. Stick figures have as much power as anything else; it's not the medium, but the resulting insight that matters.

PLAY by YOUR RULES

We've started you off with a frame for your drawing, but by all means go outside the lines! Paste over it, paint over it, draw only outside the box if you want to!

USE COLOR

Whether it's crayons, highlighters, paint, collage paper, markers – use color in your images – color helps bring your images to life.

THIS JOURNAL...

Writing Pages

Practical Pages

Checklist

WRITE FREELY

Your Wild Money Journal is a safe-haven to work through issues in your relationship with money. Honesty and compassion are your allies. If your inner critic shows up spouting negative self-talk, thank it (after all, it is on your side), and ask it to help you in a more productive way.

FILL the SPACE

Stream-of-consciousness writing is very useful for the Writing Prompts. The more you write the better chance you have of uncovering unconscious habits that keep you where you are. If you get stuck, ask yourself "Is there more?" This simple question is a powerhouse for getting at the thoughts just around the corner.

TRY IT ON

Every chapter offers practical, get-down-and-do-it exercises to build your skills and give you practice with managing your money. This is where you get to test drive new attitudes, skills and beliefs.

USE IT

Practicing new skills is awkward at first... but gets easier every time you try—so don't be afraid. We're all in this together! And if you need a little help ask Zelda! She loves to help!

Ask Zelda!

Zelda@lunajaffe.com

TRACK IT

Here you can check-in and gauge your level of completeness for each chapter. If you love checking off completed to-do items – you'll love these pages! If lists aren't really your thing, don't sweat it.

BUILD your LEXICON

The VOCAB pages for each chapter either serve to remind you of what you know, or will hopefully motivate you to learn each word listed (all of them are defined in the Field Guide starting on page 165).

Chapter 1
THE WILD MONEY PROCESS

Self-Assessment

	Wild Money Self Assessment		
1.	Right now I receive more than enough income to cover my personal expenses.	Yes	No
2.	I have a process for tracking or acknowledging the money I receive monthly.	Yes	No
3.	I feel grateful and excited about the money I receive each month.	Yes	No
4.	I understand the difference between my gross and net income.	Yes	No
5.	I express gratitude for the money that flows into my life.	Yes	No
6.	What I earn monthly is in alignment with the energy I put into the world.	Yes	No
7.	I know my Squeak-By number; what I need for basic expenses and minimum debt payments.	Yes	No
8.	I spend less than I make or receive each month.	Yes	No
9.	I feel good about the way I spend money.	Yes	No
10.	I know what my top five values are (what matters most to me), and my spending is in alignment with these values.	Yes	No
11.	I understand myself well enough to know how to avoid impulse spending.	Yes	No
12.	I pay attention to what I spend either by tracking in a check register, or by looking online every few days.	Yes	No
13.	I save at least 5% of my income monthly (into savings, retirement). (count this as a yes if you are retired)	Yes	No
14.	I know how much interest my savings are earning by percentage.	Yes	No
15.	When I use my savings for an emergency or large purchase, I replenish it as soon as possible.	Yes	No
16.	I understand my bank & brokerage statements and read them monthly.	Yes	No
17.	I can explain the difference between savings, money market and CDs.	Yes	No
18.	I have at least $5,000 in savings for emergencies or job loss.	Yes	No
19.	I can accurately define these words: stock, bond, mutual fund.	Yes	No
20.	I know the difference between dividends and interest.	Yes	No
21.	I regularly invest my money (unless retired or on disability) and/or review what I am invested in.	Yes	No
22.	I understand my own risk tolerance/comfort zone when it comes to investing..	Yes	No

23.	I know myself well enough to either invest on my own or hire an advisor/planner.	Yes	No
24.	I know how a Roth IRA works and why it's a great vehicle for retirement savings (if you are retired, answer 'yes' to this question).	Yes	No
25.	I have good health insurance for myself and my family.	Yes	No
26.	If I have dependents (kids, parents, spouse), I have at least $250k in life insurance (if you have no dependents answer "yes").	Yes	No
27.	I have either a living trust, or a will, power of attorney and advanced healthcare directive (Estate plan).	Yes	No
28.	I understand how much insurance coverage I have for my home (renters or homeowners) and car(s), and know it's enough.	Yes	No
29.	Someone other than my spouse/partner knows where I keep my important documents, and if I have them in a safe, they know how to get in.	Yes	No
30.	I have reviewed my beneficiaries on retirement, annuities, and life insurance in the past two years.	Yes	No
31.	I have a regular practice of giving money or time to those in need.	Yes	No
32.	The amount of money/time I give away is in balance with what I have to give.	Yes	No
33.	I feel good about the way I practice generosity/philanthropy.	Yes	No
34.	I understand what motivates me to donate to a particular cause.	Yes	No
35.	I have a plan for how and to whom I give money.	Yes	No
36.	I have my charitable intent written into my estate plan (will or trust).	Yes	No

Now, for each section, give yourself one point for each yes, per category:

Purple (Receive):____   Red (Spend): ____   Yellow (Nurture): ____

Green (Grow): ____   Light Blue (Protect): ____   Indigo (Give): ____

Where you are now:

0 -10 points:	**Downright Domesticated**	—Time to get to work and mend your ways.
10-20 points:	**Wandering in the Woods**	—You are headed in the right direction.
20-30 points:	**Dancing with your Wild**	—You are doing great. Keep going.
30-36 points:	**Wondrous Wild Woman**	—Call me and teach me a thing or two!

On the next page, color the petals of the mandala. If you have six points in the blue section, fill in that petal completely; if you have only one point, fill in 1/6 of the petal.

Self Assessment—Mandala Template

REFLECT

Money & Me Right Now

The assessment you just completed gives you a visual picture of how you are doing in your relationship with money. Now let's explore how this relationship feels. Put on a timer and write for 2 minutes on each of these sentence stems.

1 My relationship with money...

2 What I struggle with most in this relationship is...

3 When it comes to money, what I want most is....

CREATE

Draw or find an image that reflects your current relationship with money. Don't over analyze. What metaphor is most apt to describe this relationship? You can draw, paint, create a collage or find an image on Google, If you decide to create your images outside of this journal, consider making a color copy and pasting it in the journal so you have a record as you go through the Wild Money Process.

Title _____ *Date* _____

REFLECT

Reflect on the image you created and respond to the following questions. Are you in the picture? Is money?

1 What I notice about my image is...

2 What I like about this image is...

3 What scares me when I look at it is...

CHECKLIST

Getting Started

⚙ Set up a space in your home where you can work and play with your Wild Money Journal.

1. Get a candle and/or incense that you light only when doing the exercises in the Journal.

2. Buy or find a scarf, shawl, special sweater or other article of clothing that you put on when you sit to do this work. It's a way of marking sacred time. Put this item on before you start and then set an intention for the time you will spend on the process. When finished, remove the item and tuck it away until the next time.

3. Consider creating a playlist of music that makes you happy and hopeful. Play it at the beginning of each Wild Money session.

4. Put flowers, a favorite piece of artwork or photo of someone you admire when it comes to money near your work space.

5. Gather up your favorite art supplies, collage resources, and sources of inspiration and have them nearby for when the mood to create strikes you.

⚙ Complete the self-assessment—pg. 13

⚙ Draw your Wild Money Mandala—pg. 15

⚙ Reflect on your current relationship with money—pg. 16

⚙ Create your first image: Me and Money, right now—pg 17

⚙ Complete writing exercises reflecting on your image—pg. 18

⚙ **Celebrate!!** You have started this amazing, transformative process. You deserve this! Do something to celebrate- write yourself a thank you note, take of picture of yourself in your new space, call a friend, have a glass of wine or a cup of tea by the fire, do a little dance!

21

Chapter 2
RECEIVE MONEY WITH GRACE

CREATE

How Do You Receive?

Create or find an image that represents your current relationship to receiving money. How does your relationship look and feel right now in your life? Are there sources of income you feel great about (like work) and others that are confusing or painful (like income you receive from your ex-husband)? How might you represent those sources using a simple drawing and color? Play. Don't over think. Richness comes in the surprises that emerge.

Title _____ Date _____

REFLECT

1 Sit with your image for a few minutes. What do you notice?

2 The money I receive...

3 The way I feel when I receive my (paycheck, alimony, child support) is...

4 Truthfully, I wish I could receive...

5 Receiving money is...

6 I hate to admit it, but when it comes to money...

Money Memoir—The Cliff Notes Version

Think about significant times in your life when you received money. What stories do you carry about the ways money came into your childhood home and, more importantly, into your own hands? Write, quickly noting the scene you remember, and the resulting emotions/ conclusions.

	MEMORY	EMOTION/CONCLUSION
Money Memoir	①	
	②	
	③	
	④	
	⑤	

REFLECT

Which of these memories has the most punch or grips you in the gut with grief? Write or draw about it here. Explore what happened and why you responded the way you did.

On a separate piece of paper, write what you want to release about this experience- the feelings, the resulting stories you told yourself, whatever still plagues you.

Ritual of Release

Light a candle. Take the writing you just completed and burn it. (Careful not to burn your house down!) While it burns, release the emotion and the experience by saying, "I let go of.... I choose a new relationship with receiving money." Notice how you feel in your body as you let it go. Write about how it feels to release this story you've carried for so long.

How Big Is Your Basket?

Imagine that you have a money basket. Write for five minutes (use a timer) about your basket. Detail where it came from, how big it is, how it's decorated, and what it feels like right now. Are you carrying it? Is it on your head, or in your arms, or on the ground? Is it old or new, colorful or faded, tightly woven, or tattered and torn?

CREATE

Now create an image of the money basket you just wrote about and include yourself in the image. Think of this as your "before" picture.

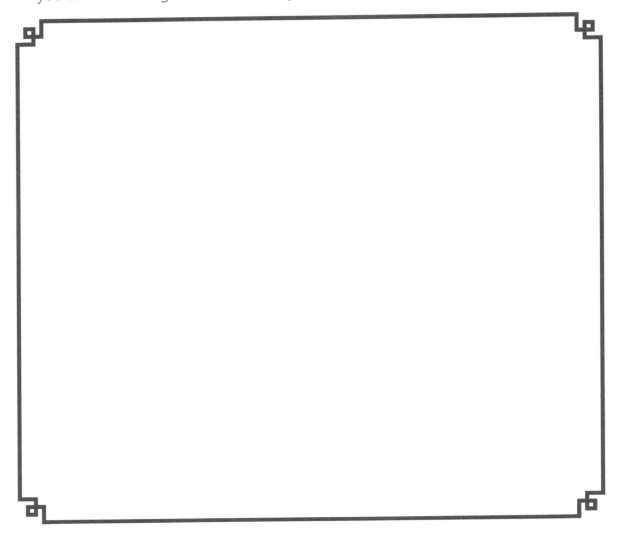

Title _____ Date _____

REFLECT

Write for five minutes about the money basket you want to have—the perfect (for you) receptacle for receiving. What is different? How does it feel? What does it look like?

CREATE

Create or find an image of your new basket. Be whimsical, powerful, and true to what would make you the happiest. Make this image one hundred percent yours.

Title _____ Date _____

A·C·T

Money In

Track all money that comes into your life: earnings, refunds, found money, interest, alimony. Note how it feels to receive this money. Do this for a month or two–long enough to see the trends and to notice when something unexpected shows up (money or feelings). A great way to track your money is to download the Wild Money Calendar at www.lunajaffe.com/calendar and use Post-Its for each day money comes in.

CIRCLE THIS MONTH
JAN FEB MAR APR
MAY JUN JUL AUG
SEP OCT NOV DEC

Tracking Money IN

AMOUNT	DATE	WHERE it CAME FROM	HOW IT FEELS TO RECEIVE it

CREATE

How Do You Receive
Part II

Look at the image you created on page 23 and search for something you can change to transform your experience of receiving. Draw this image here.

Title _____ *Date* _____

REFLECT

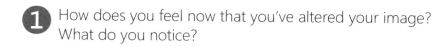

1 How does you feel now that you've altered your image?
What do you notice?

2 What would it be like to live the changes you just made in your image?

3 List five tangible things you are willing to change to express more grace when receiving money. Make them doable- small steps that you accomplish are far better than big leaps you never take!

-
-
-
-
-

36

CHECKLIST

Receive Money with Grace

⚙ Create image "How Do You Receive"—pg. 23

⚙ Reflect on your image—pg. 24

⚙ Complete Money Memoir chart—pg. 27

⚙ Reflect on one significant money memory—pg. 28

⚙ Ritual of Release—pg. 29

⚙ How Big is your Basket—pg. 30

⚙ Create a Money Basket image and reflection—pg. 31

⚙ Create a new image of your Money Basket—pg. 33

⚙ Complete Money In exercise; create a calendar! —pg. 34

⚙ Create image "How Do You Receive Part II"—pg. 35

⚙ Reflect on your new image—pg. 36

VOCABULARY

IF YOU KNOW IT, CHECK IT OFF! IF YOU DON'T, WRITE IN THE DEFINITION FROM THE FIELD GUIDE!

- ⚙ Asset

- ⚙ Capital Gain and Capital Loss

- ⚙ Compound and Simple Interest

- ⚙ Cost Basis

- ⚙ Equity

- ⚙ Fixed Income

- ⚙ HELOC (Home Equity Line of Credit)

- ⚙ Index

- ⚙ Liquidity

- ⚙ Margin Loan

- ⚙ Net Worth

- ⚙ Portfolio

- ⚙ Registration

39

chronicle * intentions * observations * scribbles * meditations * reverie * reflections * Musings * thoughts * diary * journal *

Chapter 3
SPEND WITH INTENTION

CREATE

Tending Your Forest

What does your financial forest look like? Imagine it. Are there towering old growth trees (money you inherited), or is the forest newly planted and just taking root? Are you spending (harvesting) resources you carefully nurtured, or are you cutting willy-nilly in a frenzy of spending, blind to the desolation you are creating for yourself?

Draw or find an image of your relationship with spending,.

Title _____ *Date* _____

REFLECT

1 It's easy for me to spend money on...

2 I never spend money (but wish I would/could) on...

3 When it comes to money, I struggle with...

4 It pisses me off when my partner/spouse/child/friend spends money on...

5 When I consider why that makes me mad, I realize...

6 I am getting better, especially when it comes to...

7 If I could change one thing about my relationship with spending...

A C T

From Squeaking By to Living with Plenty

It's time to look at where you stand, financially, by evaluating your spending, and then find resonance by aligning your spending with your values. No matter what your imagination is telling you, the empowerment that comes from knowing where you stand beats the shame, fear, and imagined worst-case-scenarios of not knowing.

Gather these materials:

- 3 highlighters (different colors)
- Pencil & eraser
- Bank statements (last 6 months)
- Check register
- Calculator
- Art supplies (need to make this fun!)
- Credit card statements

Schedule about 2 hours when you know you'll be at peak energy and won't be distracted or disturbed.
(Unless it's by a loved one offering a pep-talk or snacks)

How do you know if an expense is Squeak-By, Enough, or Plenty? The chart below breaks it down for you.

	Squeak-By	Enough	Plenty
Savings	$0	$200	$500
Haircut	$30 (cheapest haircut possible)	$60 (going to the stylist you want)	$100 (extras, color, highlights)
Credit Card Debt	$25 (minimum monthly payment)	$100 (more than minimum per month)	$0 (no credit card debt)
Cable TV	$0 (don't have cable)	$60 (basic cable)	$100 (all the channels)

ACT

1️⃣ Starting at Squeak-By

Your Squeak-By number is important to know, no matter which level you're currently operating at. Squeak-By is the amount of money that is necessary for you to pay basic needs and obligations.

Perhaps you've gotten used to a level of comfort that feels like you "can't live without," but if put into a tight enough bind, you would be able to squeak-by without the data plan, cable TV, or eating out. You still have to pay the minimum on your credit card though.

Use the three highlighters to go through your statements and mark purchases as they fall into each Category: SQUEAK-BY, ENOUGH, PLENTY.

TRAN. DATE	DESCRIPTION	DEPOSITS	WITHDRAWALS	BALANCE
12/03	CHECK # 001059 *rent*		$ 950.00	$2,574.74
12/04	WITHDRAWAL DEBIT CARD CO: BURGERVILLE		$ 11.00	$2,563.74
12/11	WITHDRAWAL ACH AD&D WIRELESS TYPE: ADN WEBPAY ID: 00170075145		$ 105.36	$2,458.38
12/15	WITHDRAWAL DEBIT CARD CO: MEXICAN VILLA RENTALS		$ 250.00	$2,208.38
12/17	WITHDRAWAL DEBIT CARD CO: OMEGA AIRLINES *visit home*		$ 576.00	$1,632.38
12/19	RECURRING WITHDRAWAL DEBIT CARD ALEDA FITNESS WWW.ALEDAFITNESS.C OR		$ 189.00	$1,443.38
12/20	CHECK # 001058 *water bill*		$ 271.00	$1,172.38
12/21	WITHDRAWAL UONLINE TRANSFER TO SHARE 13 MTHLY SVGS FOR HOUSE DOWNPAYMENT		$ 350.00	$ 822.38
12/23	DEPOSIT CASH	$1,259.00		$2,081.38
12/26	WITHDRAWAL DEBIT CARD TYPE: INS PREM ID: 1731282686 *Renter's Insurance*		$ 15.00	$2,066.38

SQUEAK-BY   ENOUGH   PLENTY

46

This page is yours to use for figuring out how much of your bills are really Squeak-By vs. Enough. You can calculate the monthly cost of quarterly or annual bills or make notes about upcoming expenses.

If your numbers vary wildly from month to month, average them.

If you had to strip down to the most basic phone plan, what would your monthly obligation cost?

Saving money doesn't happen when you are just squeaking by, but definitely needs to be included in your Enough numbers.).

Still not sure which category a charge is? How does it feel? Is it an obligation (Squeak-By), an extra (Enough), or a luxury (Plenty)?

A C T

② **Determine your Expenses**

Use the information from your highlighted statements and the worksheet (p. 47) to fill in the chart on the next page with your Squeak-By, Enough and Plenty numbers.

›HOUSING‹
RENT
MORTGAGE
PROP. TAXES
GARDEN
IMPROVEMENTS
DECOR

›DEBTS‹
MEDICAL
LOANS
– STUDENT
– VEHICLE
– OTHER
CREDIT CARDS
STORE CARDS

›UTILITIES‹
ELECTRICITY
GAS
OIL (HEAT)
WATER/SEWER
GARBAGE
BASIC PHONE

›EXTRA UTILS.‹
CABLE
ENTERTAINMENT
SUBSCRIPTIONS
INTERNET
CELL PHONE
– DATA

›INSURANCES‹
HOME/RENTER'S
VEHICLE INS.
HEALTH INS.
LIFE INSURANCE

›FOOD‹
GROCERIES
EATING OUT
FINE DINING
CONVENIENCE
CAFÉS

›TRANSPORT‹
MAINTENANCE
FUEL
PARKING/TOLLS
PUBLIC TRANSIT

›CHILDREN‹
SCHOOL FEES
EXTRA ACTIVITIES
ALLOWANCE
CLOTHING
OTHER

›PETS‹
FOOD
VET
TOYS

Circle the categories that apply to YOUR spending and write them in on the chart on the following page.

›PERSONAL‹
HAIR CUT/CARE
BOOKS
MUSIC
CLOTHING
ART SUPPLIES
TECHNOLOGY
DATES/ADVENTURE

›HEALTH CARE‹
DOCTOR
DENTIST
OPTOMETRIST
MASSAGE
ACUPUNCTURE
YOGA/EXERCISE
HEALTH CLUB
THERAPY
PRESCRIPTIONS
SUPPLEMENTS

›SAVINGS‹
EMERGENCY
RETIREMENT
TRAVEL
COLLEGE
OTHER

A C T

Intentional Spending Chart

CATEGORY / NEW NAME	SQUEAK BY	ENOUGH	PLENTY
TOTAL			

Write your core values (p. 50) and assign each value a color.

To download this chart, go to lunajaffe.com/templates.

③ Name Your Core Values

◎ Look at the values below and write the 6-8 values that resonate most deeply with you (even if at the moment you're not putting time, energy, or money in that direction).

◎ Where are these values reflected in your spending? Assign each value a color and write them in the box on the opposite page. Then underline each expense that expresses that value (some might represent two!)

If you're just squeaking-by and missing values from your list, it's time to brainstorm the ways you can express those values for free.

50

A C T

④ Renaming Your Spending Categories

You receive a benefit from each expense, yet it's easy to take the most basic expenses (like utilities) for granted. They may not feel like they relate to one of your values, but they provide comfort and ease, even security. You may end up realizing security is more important than you thought.

⑥ Become more aligned with your spending by renaming your categories to something that will make you smile each time you see it. "Emergency Savings" could change into "Peace of Mind." "Housing" might feel more aligned if you rename it to "My Nest," or "Home Sweet Home."

Notice on the Intentional Spending Chart on page 49, there is room for renaming your spending categories with your new more awesome names.

⑤ Dreaming Up Plenty

Set aside numbers for a moment and let your imagination run away with you. This is an area for you to think big. Now bigger. Tap into your heart and really open up to the possibility that your dream is coming true. What would living the dream look like to you?

Brainstorm a list of things, experiences and opportunities you want in your life.

53

⑥ Choose 3-5 of your favorite "Plenty" items from the previous pages. Fill in the chart below with the benefit, cost, and time frame you'd like the item within, and what that equates to on a monthly basis.

⑥ Put these items and numbers into your spending chart on page 49.

LIVING with PLENTY

DREAM	BENEFIT	COST	TIME FRAME	$/MONTH To SAVE

A C T

⑥ Putting It All Together

Great Job. You've done so much! You've...

- ⊚ analyzed your current spending
- ⊚ broken out your Squeak-By and Enough numbers
- ⊚ identified your values
- ⊚ matched up your spending with those values
- ⊚ figured out ways to fulfill any currently missing values.

Not to mention, you dreamed big and put your dreams in your plan!

Next Steps...

This is no one-night-stand! You will need to revisit these numbers by making a living document that works with your life and your brain.

You've done the hard work of looking at what you need and want in your life. You are on the road to plenty and you're ready to transfer your numbers to a budgeting system.

> If you like the paper and pencil method, you can find this document for download at www.lunajaffe.com/templates
>
> —OR—
>
> You could set up an Excel spreadsheet following your final chart.
>
> —OR—
>
> My favorite electronic program is called You Need A Budget (www.ynab.com). It's very approachable and they have free webinars and great support. You can even customize your categories so they align with your values. Sweet!

REFLECT

1 Squeaking By is...

2 When I think about having Enough, I...

3 What scares me when I look at these numbers is...

4 What I realize about myself is...

5 When it comes to having Plenty, what surprises me is...

REFLECT

How Feelings Impact Spending

Mindmap the way your feelings and emotions impact how and when you spend your money. Be sure to include positive feelings as well as emotions that are triggered by external events like a relationship ending, major stress at work, dealing with an ailing parent, or your partner's decision to leave a lucrative job to start a business. If you are uncertain of how to do a mind map, please refer to page 162.

1 Write down 7 emotions (both positive and negative) you experience in your own life.

2 Place each word in one of the small circles on the next page. On the lines radiating out, name how you spend money when feeling that emotion.

How My Feelings Impact My Spending

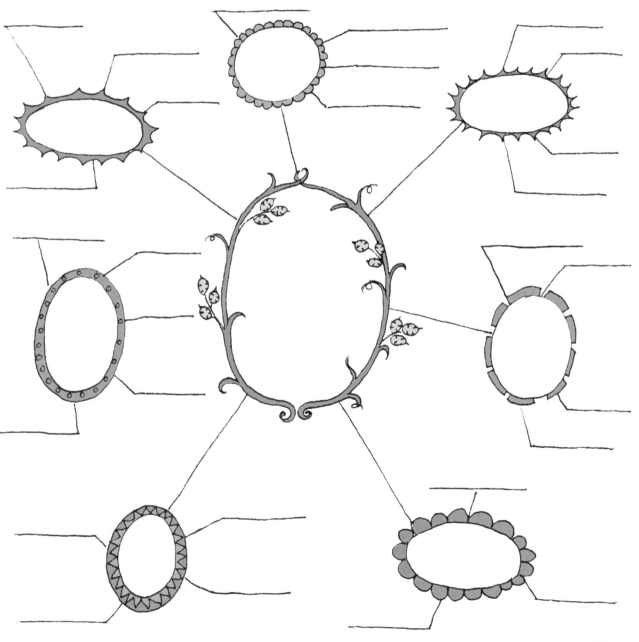

REFLECT

REFLECT on your mindmap:

1 When I feel good about my life and myself I spend money on...

2 When I feel bad or anxious, I buy... and then I feel....

3 When I look this mind map, I feel....

4 Which emotion is most difficult to deal with, when it comes to money?

5 When you are feeling this way, what do you need most?

6 What question might you ask yourself before you spend money that will help you become aware of what you are feeling?

WHAT IS THIS REALLY COSTING ME?

CREATE

A New Vision of Spending

Create or find an image of how you want your relationship with spending money to be as you move forward. Consider your work with Enough and Plenty, and the exploration of your values. What does it look like to feel firmly rooted in a practice of sustainable spending?

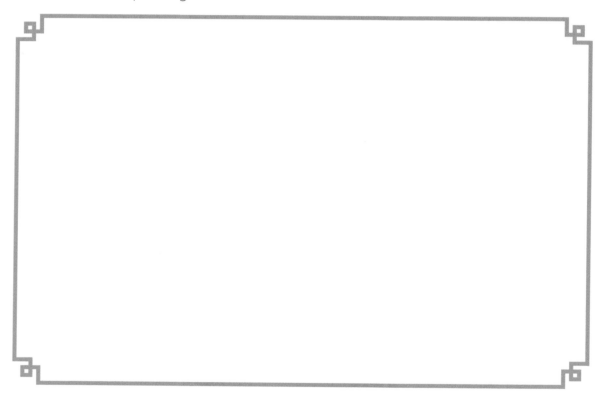

Title _____ *Date* _____

REFLECT

1 How does this image feel to you?

2 How is it different from the first image? Notice changes in color, relationship, and where you are in the picture (if at all).

For fun, go to a copy shop and reduce this image to the size of a wallet photo; keep it next to your credit/debit cards as a reminder of the life you desire to live.

CHECKLIST

Spend with Intention

- Create first spending image—pg. 43
- Reflect on your image—pg.44
- From Squeaking-By to Living with Plenty—pg. 45
  1. Starting at Squeak-By—pg. 46
  2. Determine your expenses—pg. 48
  3. Name your core values—pg. 50
  4. Rename your spending categories—pg. 51
  5. Dreaming up plenty—pg. 52
  6. Putting it all together—pg. 55
- Reflect—pg. 56
- Create a Mindmap of "How Feelings Impact Spending"—pg. 57
- Reflect on your Mindmap—pg. 59
- Create a new vision of your relationship with spending—pg. 61
- Reflect on your new image—pg. 62

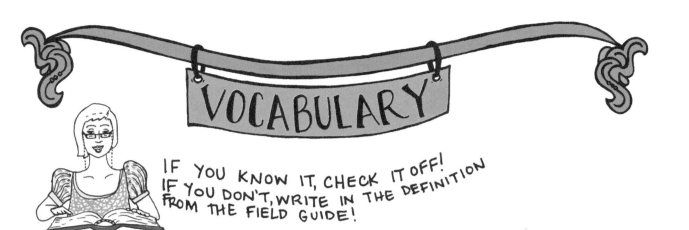

VOCABULARY

IF YOU KNOW IT, CHECK IT OFF!
IF YOU DON'T, WRITE IN THE DEFINITION
FROM THE FIELD GUIDE!

- ○ Dividends

- ○ Dollar Cost Averaging (DCA)

- ○ Dow Jones Industrial Average (DJIA)

- ○ Interest

- ○ Initial Public Offering (IPO)

- ○ Rate of Return

- ○ Risk Tolerance/Comfort Zone

- ○ Roth IRA and contribution limits

- ○ S & P 500

- ○ Tax Deferred

- ○ Tax Loss Harvesting

- ○ Taxable Account

- ○ Traditional IRA and contribution limits

- ○ Yield

66

Chapter 4
NURTURE YOUR NEST EGG

CREATE

Nurture or Neglect?

Create an image that represents how you nurture your nest egg. Where are you in relationship to your nest egg? Are you sitting on it, ignoring it, or neglecting it? Do you have any savings? Are you even aware it's your job to protect it? Have you put others in charge of tending it? How is that working out? Let an image come and simply draw it (or find an image) without over analyzing.

 Title _____  Date _____

REFLECT

1 What I notice when I look at my image is...

2 What surprises me is...

3 When I look at my nest egg, I feel...

4 I got to this place with my nest egg...

REFLECT

Nest Egg Dialogue

Assume for a moment that your nest egg can talk. Ask it a few questions and see what it has to tell you. Be curious and ask any question that pops into your head.

You:

Nest Egg:

You:

Nest Egg:

You:

Nest Egg:

You:

Nest Egg:

You:

Nest Egg:

You:

Nest Egg:

You:

REFLECT

1 Re-read your dialogue. Circle the statements that have punch or power for you.

Rewrite them here:

2 What is one action your nest egg suggested (or demanded?).

3 What would it be like to follow through on her suggestions?

REFLECT

1. What was your experience with saving as a child?

2. Did your parents/grandparents save? Invest? How did they impact you?

3. Who set the bar for savings in your life, and what did you learn from them?

4. Imagine having $10,000 in a savings account. How do you feel?

5. If I really tell the truth, the way I feel about saving money is...

6. The hardest thing about saving is...

7. When it comes to saving, what I feel hopeful about is...

BUILD & GROW your NEST EGG in 8 SIMPLE STEPS

1 EMERGENCY SAVINGS
I have $ _____ CURRENTLY SAVED UP. _____ date
☐ I'LL COMMIT $ _____ /MONTH TOWARDS SAVINGS. _____ date
☐ I HAVE $1,000 ALL SAVED UP! _____ date

2 ELIMINATE CONSUMER DEBT
I'm burdened with $ _____ IN CONSUMER DEBT. _____ date
☐ I'LL COMMIT $ _____ /MONTH TOWARD THIS DEBT. _____ date
☐ I'M ALL PAID OFF TO $0.00! _____ date

3 INCREASE SAVINGS
I have $ _____ CURRENTLY SAVED UP. _____ date
☐ I'LL COMMIT $ _____ /MONTH TOWARD THIS GOAL. _____ date
☐ I HAVE $5,000 ALL SAVED UP! _____ date

4 EMPLOYER'S RETIREMENT PLAN
☐ I'M CONTRIBUTING _____ % PER MONTH. _____ date
☐ _____ % GETTING FULL COMPANY MATCH _____ date
☐ N/A *because* _____

5 PERSONAL RETIREMENT PLAN
☐ I'M CONTRIBUTING $ _____ /MONTH _____ date
☐ FULLY FUNDED THIS YEAR @ $5,500 ($6,500 if OVER 50) _____ date
☐ N/A *or* RETIRED

6 INCREASE RETIREMENT SAVINGS
☐ FULLY FUNDED THIS YEAR @ $17,500 ($23,000 if OVER 50) _____ date
☐ N/A *because* _____

7 INVESTING
☐ I'M AUTOMATICALLY INVESTING $ _____ /MONTH _____ date

8 COLLEGE SAVINGS FOR KIDS
☐ I'LL COMMIT $ _____ /MONTH TOWARD 529 PLAN _____ date
☐ N/A *because* _____

CREATE

Re-Vision Your Nest Egg

Make a new image of your nest egg. Imagine you have emergency cash, no debt other than your mortgage, a substantial retirement account, and investments outside of retirement (stocks, real estate, business). How do you feel? What does that look like? What helps you to feel safe, in control, and secure? Put all of that into your image.

Title _____ Date _____

CHECKLIST

Nurture Your Nest Egg

✳ Spend a little time improving your organization of bills or the place where you work on bills. Is it beautiful? Are you remembering to light a candle or incense? How can you add joy?

✳ Create the image "Nurture or Neglect"—pg. 69

✳ Reflect on your current nest egg—pg. 70

✳ Complete the Nest Egg dialogue—pg. 71

✳ Reflect on the Nest Egg dialogue—pg. 72

✳ Write about your experiences with saving money—pg. 73

✳ Grow your nest egg—pg. 76

✳ Create the image "Revision Your Nest Egg"—pg. 77

✳ Review your bank accounts. Do you understand the statements? Do you like the bank and the experience you've had there? If not, consider changing to a local bank or credit union. Here is a list of things you might ask when thinking about a change:

~ *Statements:* Ask to see a sample statement. Can you read it? You want to bank somewhere that has a clear statement!

~*Online Banking:* Can you easily do bill pay, transfer money, check balances from a mobile device?

~*Fees:* What are the fees associated with any accounts you might open? Do they reimburse ATM fees? Are there bank locations and ATMS close by where you live and work?

~*Overdraft Protection:* make sure you have it!

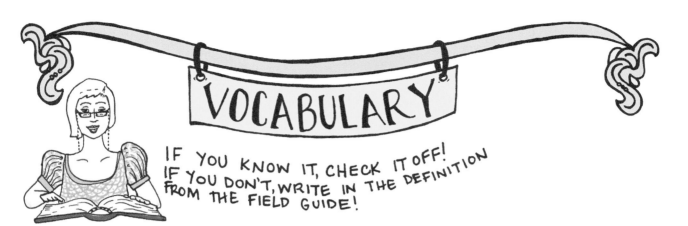

VOCABULARY

IF YOU KNOW IT, CHECK IT OFF!
IF YOU DON'T, WRITE IN THE DEFINITION FROM THE FIELD GUIDE!

- Certificate of Deposit (CD)

- FDIC insurance

- SIPC

- FINRA

- SEC

- 401k

- 403b

- SEP IRA

- SIMPLE IRA

- Money Market Account

- APR (used when describing interest rates)

- YTD

Chapter 5
GROW YOUR GOLD

CREATE

How Does Your Garden Grow?

Create or find an image that represents your current relationship with investing using the garden metaphor. Is it a vibrant, diverse, well-tended garden or are things dying on the vine? Is the soil rich and full of nutrients, or rock-hard clay?

Title _____ Date _____

REFLECT

1 When I think about my garden/investments I feel...

2 In my family investing was...

3 What scares me most about investing my money is...

4 The best financial investment I ever made was—because...

5 If I had an extra $5,000 every month I would invest in...

Diary of My Disasters

What experiences have you had with investing? What was the result? Most importantly, what conclusion did you make based on these experiences? (Don't forget to include family members whose investing experiences impacted you either directly or indirectly.)

diary of my DISASTERS		
DECISION	RESULT	CONCLUSION MADE
①		
②		
③		
④		
⑤		

REFLECT

Select one of these experiences and write about it for five to ten minutes. Describe what happened and the circumstances surrounding it. What did you feel at the time? Who or what was influencing you? What story have you perpetuated as a result of this experience?

A C T

Ritual:

On a separate piece of paper write down the negative conclusions you made about yourself and your ability to invest wisely and with confidence. Take this page, write 'Thank You, I Release You," across it, and then burn or bury it. Notice how you feel.

Rewrite Your Story

Now write the antidote to these negative conclusions. For example, "I suck at investing" might become, "I am capable of learning to invest skillfully."

Old Conclusion:_____

New Affirmation: _____

Old Conclusion:_____

New Affirmation: _____

Old Conclusion:_____

New Affirmation: _____

Comfort Zone Quiz

1. How do you drive?

a. Typically I drive 5 miles over the speed limit.
b. I obey the speed limit, or go slower—people are crazy out there!
c. As fast as I can without getting caught.
d. I do as other people do, might be 10 mph over the speed limit or more, just depends.

2. If you unexpectedly received $30,000 to invest, what would you do?

a. Deposit it in a savings account or CD and leave it there—better safe than sorry, right?
b. Invest in a portfolio of stocks or stock mutual funds, and commit to leaving it there for 3-5 years.
c. Invest in high quality bonds or bond mutual funds, earn a little interest.
d. Invest it all in one killer stock you've been following for the past year.

3. You are on Jeopardy and can choose one of the following. Which would you take?

a. $1,000 in cash prizes.
b. A 10% chance of winning $100,000.
c. A 30% chance of winning $10,000.
d. A 50% chance of winning $2,000.

4. You have just finished saving for an "once-in-a-lifetime" vacation. Three weeks before your departure date, you lose your job. Would you:

a. Cancel the vacation and look for a job.
b. Pack for months instead of weeks, because now you finally have time to see the world.
c. Go as scheduled, reasoning that you need the time to prepare for the job search.
d. Take a much more modest vacation.

5. In general, how would your best friend describe you as a risk taker?

a. Adventurous, courageous, trusting of the outcome.
b. Cautious, always considering the worst case scenario.
c. Willing to take risks after completing adequate research.
d. Downright nuts; an adrenaline junkie.

6. How comfortable are you investing in stocks or stock mutual funds?

a. Love it, bring it on.
b. Fairly comfortable, like driving in the snow... I can do it if I have to.
c. Not comfortable at all.
d. I have never invested in the stock market.

7. When you think of the word "risk" which of the following words comes to mind first?

a. Loss
b. Uncertainty
c. Opportunity
d. Thrill

8. You are in Hawaii for the first time. Where are you comfortable?

a. Swimming in the ocean, body surfing, boogie boarding.
b. On the balcony of my ocean view hotel room—you never know when a tsunami might hit.
c. In the water, with my feet touching the sandy bottom.
d. On a lounge chair on the beach—the water looks beautiful from here!

9. The stock market is fluctuating wildly, economic news is bleak and your friends are freaking out. Assume you have at least $40k invested right now. How would you behave?

a. I'd shove all my brokerage statements into a file, unopened and stay the course.
b. I'd open my statements, fret, call my advisor every week for reassurance, and maybe move to a more conservative portfolio.
c. I would believe what I hear, move everything to cash and sleep better at night.
d. I'm a rebel, so I would take any spare money I have and buy stock while it's cheap.

10. Suppose your great aunt left you an inheritance of $100,000, stipulating in her will that you invest ALL the money in ONE of the following choices. Which one would you select?

a. A portfolio of 15 common stocks.
b. A savings account or money market fund.
c. A mutual fund portfolio of stocks and bonds.
d. I would invest in my best friend's start-up, it's going to be amazing!

To score this quiz: For each question note the points given for each of your answers and write them in the space provided.

1.	a) 3	b) 4	c) 1	d) 2	2.	a) 4	b) 2	c) 3	d) 1
3.	a) 4	b) 1	c) 2	d) 3	4.	a) 4	b) 1	c) 2	d) 3
5.	a) 2	b) 4	c) 3	d) 1	6.	a) 1	b) 2	c) 3	d) 4
7.	a) 4	b) 3	c) 2	d) 1	8.	a) 1	b) 4	c) 2	d) 3
9.	a) 2	b) 3	c) 4	d) 1	10.	a) 2	b) 4	c) 3	d) 1

1._____   2._____   3._____   4._____   5._____
6._____   7._____   8._____   9._____   10._____

YOUR TOTAL SCORE:_____

Visualize Your Comfort Zone

STABLE: 32-40 points. Your mantra is...

"I don't care if I make money, just don't want to lose any."

GROUNDED: 26-33 points. Your mantra is...

"I want a little growth, as long as it doesn't freak me out."

BRANCHING OUT: 18-25 points. Your mantra is...

"I'm in for the long haul, don't mind a few storms if I have more at the end."

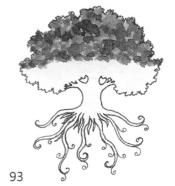

FLYING IN THE WIND. 10-17 points. Your mantra is...

"I enjoy adventure and possibility, and have confidence I'll recover even if a big storm hits."

CREATE

Draw your Comfort Zone on this tree and write your thoughts here.

ACT

Investing in Your Comfort Zone

Do this exercise if you have any savings or investments— If you have a 401k, Roth IRA, rental house, stock account (including stock purchase plan at work), CD at the bank, savings bonds, gold bullion, etc.

Use this form to determine how your current assets are invested:

Portfolio Portrait: CURRENT ALLOCATION					
ACCOUNT	STABLE	CONSERVATIVE	MODERATE	GROWTH	AGGRESSIVE
ROTH, TRAD IRA, 401(k), 403(b), BROKERAGE, BANK	CASH & EQUIVALENTS	BONDS, SAVINGS BONDS	G/I STOCKS, RENTAL PROPERTY	GROWTH STOCKS, PROPERTY (NON-RENTAL)	SMALL CAP STOCKS, HIGH TECH, NEW COMPANIES, GOLD/SILVER
TOTAL:					

Add Stable + Conservative Numbers   **Add Moderate Growth + Aggressive Growth Numbers**

Add Both Subtotals to get Denominator

(total value of your portfolio)

$$\frac{\rule{2cm}{0pt}}{\rule{2cm}{0pt}} = 0.\_\_ \rightarrow \rule{1.5cm}{0pt} \%$$ (in stable/conservative investments)

$$\frac{\rule{2cm}{0pt}}{\rule{2cm}{0pt}} = 0.\_\_ \rightarrow \rule{1.5cm}{0pt} \%$$ (in moderate/aggressive growth investments)

A C T

Color in the tree on the left to reflect your comfort zone as discovered on page 93. Your current portfolio will be reflected in the way you color the tree on the right.

FLYING IN the WIND		D		100%
BRANCHING OUT		C		80%/20%
GROUNDED		B		50%/50%
STABLE		A		100%

Comfort Zone   *Current Allocation*

Are your trees the same or wildly different? What do you notice?

Remember: You change your investment allocation to fit your comfort zone, not the other way around.

REFLECT

How are you feeling, right now, about your relationship with money?

(Write, draw or collage here)

REFLECT

Your Body as Co-Pilot

1 Take a deep, full-body breath, allowing your belly to expand. Do this several times until you feel centered.

2 What decision (financial or otherwise) have you made in the past five years that you feel really good about? You trusted yourself and had a great outcome. Maybe you asked for a raise and received it or gracefully managed your mother's estate. Write about it.

3 Do you recall how you felt in your body when you were making this decision, or after it was made? Describe it.

REFLECT

My great decision...

HOW DID MY GREAT DECISION FEEL?

RAISED MY HOURLY RATE 20% AND MY CLIENTS RESPONDED "IT'S ABOUT TIME"

HOW DOES THIS FEEL?

CURRENT DECISION

LIKE THIS

4 Write your decision in the circle above. It'll be your baseline comparison for the Body as Co-Pilot technique.

5 Decorate both circles – you can use them each time you need to make an important financial decision.

When you have an important financial decision to make:

6 Close your eyes, place your hand on the great decision circle. Remember how it felt when you really listened and made that good decision.

7 Now, move your hand to the second circle. Listen deeply for anxiety -or- congruence -or- angst -or- peacefulness. Jot down the feelings you notice.

8 How else do you check-in with yourself around important financial decisions? Making a great financial decision involves:

CREATE

A New Relationship
With Investing

Create or find an image that reflects your new perspective and intention for your relationship with growing your gold.

𝒯itle _____ 𝒟ate _____

REFLECT

1 What's different about this image from the first one you created on page 85?

2 Learning about investing...

3 What makes me most anxious (excited, afraid, curious) about investing is...

4 If I really tell the truth, I...

5 What I'm aware of right now is...

A C T

What are three concrete steps you can take to begin to embody this new relationship with investing? Did you decide you need an advisor? Is it time to set-up a monthly investing program? Need a second opinion? Be specific—who will you see, when will you open that account and start funding it?

1

2

3

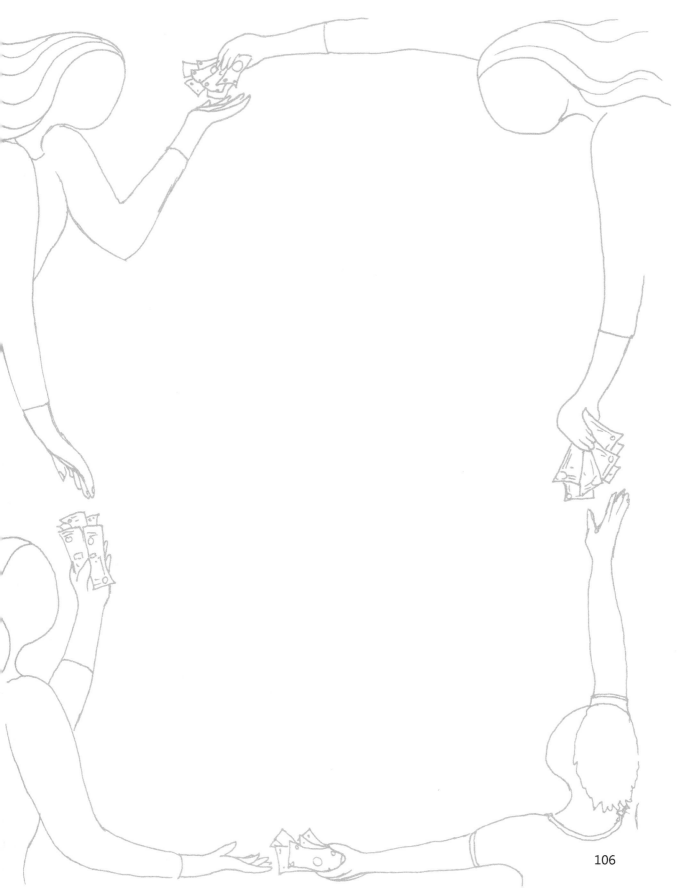

CHECKLIST

Grow Your Gold

☼ If you have brokerage or retirement plan statements, organize them in files—Make sure to open every envelope. Throw away old prospectuses and annual reports (over 1 year old)

☼ Create the image "How Does Your Garden Grow"—pg. 85

☼ Reflect on your image—pg. 86

☼ Complete "Diary of my Disasters"—pg. 87

☼ Ritual and re-writing your story—pg. 89

☼ Complete the Comfort Zone Quiz—pg. 91

☼ Investing in your Comfort Zone—pg. 95

☼ Complete Your Body as Co-Pilot exercise—pg. 98

☼ Create an image of your new relationship with investing—pg. 103

☼ Complete writing exercise—pg. 104

☼ Take action! Write three steps you will take to move forward—pg. 105

☼ **Celebrate,** again!! You are more than half way done! Bravo! Do something sweet for yourself. Acknowledge yourself for your commitment and desire to learn.

☼ **Send me an email and tell me you completed this step, and I'll send you a handwritten postcard! luna@lunajaffe.com, or snail mail (which I love!) 7837 SW Capitol Hwy, Portland, OR 97219, USA**

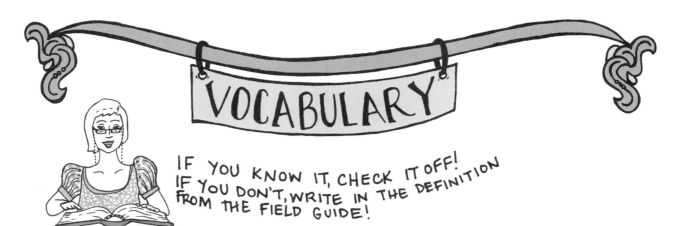

VOCABULARY

IF YOU KNOW IT, CHECK IT OFF! IF YOU DON'T, WRITE IN THE DEFINITION FROM THE FIELD GUIDE!

- ✺ Stock

- ✺ Bond

- ✺ Mutual Fund

- ✺ Growth and Income

- ✺ Growth

- ✺ Aggressive Growth

- ✺ Corporate vs. Municipal vs. Government Bonds

- ✺ High Yield vs. Investment Grade

- ✺ Maturity (related to bonds)

- ✺ Small, Mid, Large Cap Stock

- ✺ Global vs. International Mutual Fund

- ✺ Diversification

- ✺ Asset Allocation

- ✺ Fund Manager

Chapter 6
PROTECT YOUR WILD PLACES

CREATE!

How Do You Protect Yourself and Your Loved Ones?

Create an image that reflects how you currently protect yourself and your loved ones, both your income and your assets.

Title _____ Date _____

REFLECT

1. Pause for a moment and look at your image. What do you feel when you look at it?

2. What do you notice in the image?

3. When I think about protecting my money/assets, I....

4. Insurance is...

5. The honest truth is, that when it comes to protecting my assets, I...

6. Estate planning is...

7. Getting things in order so that my loved ones are protected is...

CREATE

Calling On Your Protector

Your protector is the part of you that values your dreams, knows what you've worked for, and who you love. Your protector self is proactive and clear-headed; she fiercely loves you and wants to ensure that you and your loved ones are well cared for. It's time to evoke her presence in your life.

Draw or find an image of your protector-self and give her a name.

Title _____ Date _____

Write a letter from your protector to yourself. Let her tell you everything about how it has been trying to protect you and your assets during the past few decades.

Dear _____

ACT

Read back through what you wrote and underline or circle a few key messages that you want to explore further. The truth is that we need protection sometimes, and knowing this power is within, can help motivate you to take action, like drawing up a will, or finally getting life insurance.

My Protector's Key Messages to Me:

2

3

I'm willing to TAKE ACTION! Here's what I can do right now....

Take the image of your protector and the letter she wrote you and hang it up so you will be frequently reminded of the strength and power you have on your side.

REFLECT

A History of Protection

REFLECT on your experiences both as a child and as an adult. What do you remember about how you were (or weren't) protected from disaster?

REFLECT

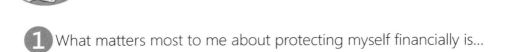

1 What matters most to me about protecting myself financially is...

2 What I remember about the ways I was protected as a child is....

3 When trauma/ tragedy/ misfortune struck in my family, we...

4 My beliefs about protecting myself/ my family come from...

5 The way my parents communicated their wishes to me was...

6 My biggest challenge when it comes to protecting my income/ assets is...

TAKE INVENTORY

	DOCUMENT/TYPE	NEED IT?	HAVE IT? Y	HAVE IT? N	COMMENTS/NOTES
Estate Plan	LIVING TRUST				
	WILL				
	POWER of ATTORNEY				
	HEALTHCARE DIRECTIVE				
	BENEFICIARIES CURRENT				
Insurance	AUTO INSURANCE				
	HOME or RENTERS				
	LIFE INSURANCE				
	HEALTH INSURANCE				
	DENTAL INSURANCE				
	DISABILITY LONG TERM SHORT TERM				
	UMBRELLA INSURANCE				
	LONG TERM CARE				

Key
☐ ESSENTIAL
☐ ADD AS YOU CAN AFFORD IT

CREATE

In the Circle of Protection

Imagine that you have your estate plan and insurance in place, your loved ones know where to find things and why you made the decisions that you did. What does it feel like to know that you can weather the storms, have reserves in case of illness, and that your treasured possessions will go where you want them to go? Create or find an image of that reflects this feeling of having your plan of protection in place.

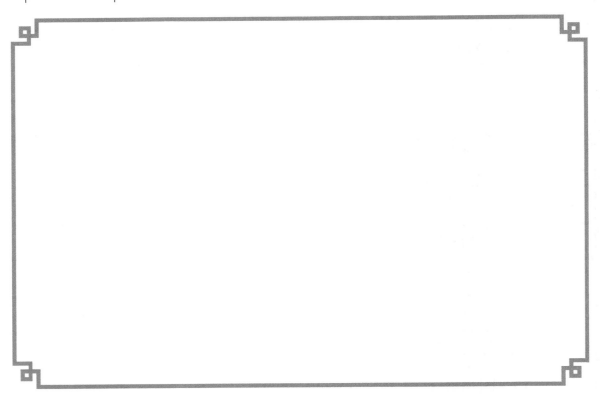

Title _____ *Date* _____

REFLECT

What I notice about my image is...

What are your next steps? Which pieces do you need to attend to right away?

1

2

3

What might get in your way of doing this? Name three things that could derail you from completing your next steps. How will you deal with each of these potential roadblocks? Write down at least one antidote to counter each roadblock.

1

2

3

REWARD YOURSELF!! Determine a reward that you will give yourself or your family once you have completed this step. For example, complete the estate plan, take the family on a vacation; Get life insurance in place, give yourself $250 for new clothes, or sign up for that pottery class you always wanted to take.

My reward for completing these steps will be _____

FOR the RECORD
WHAT YOUR LOVED ONES NEED TO KNOW WHEN YOU CAN'T TELL THEM

ESTATE PLANNING ESSENTIALS

WILL/TRUST
WILL/TRUST DOCUMENTS

LETTERS of INSTRUCTION with LIST of FRIENDS/FAM ADVISORS to CALL IMMEDIATELY

PERSONAL LETTERS to CHILDREN

LIST of ALL PASSWORDS especially
• PHONE
• COMPUTER
• FINANCIAL ACCOUNTS

IDENTITY DOCUMENTS copy of
• BIRTH CERT.
• SOCIAL SEC. CARD
• CREDIT CARDS

PROOF OF OWNERSHIP

DEEDS
• REAL ESTATE
• LAND
• CEMETARY

MORTGAGE
MORTGAGE INFORMATION

PROOF OF
• LOANS MADE
• DEBTS OWED

CARS, etc
VEHICLE TITLES

INVESTMENTS
• BROKERAGE ACCOUNTS
• STOCK CERTIFICATES
• SAVINGS BONDS

OPERATING AGREEMENTS
• BUSINESS PARTNERSHIPS
• CORPORATE

TAX DOCUMENTS
RETURNS for PAST 2-4 YEARS

BANK ACCOUNTS

LIST of BANK ACCTS including HOW THEY ARE TITLED JOINT, TRUST ETC.

LIST of ALL BANK LOGINS
• USERNAME
• PASSWORDS

LIST of SAFE DEPOSIT BOXES and KEYS

MEDICAL

MEDICAL HISTORY
• PERSONAL
• FAMILY
• PET/VET INFO.

HIPPA FORMS to GIVE AUTHORIZATION to RELEASE HEALTH CARE INFORMATION

LIVING WILL -or- ADVANCED HEALTH CARE DIRECTIVE (for THE STATES WHERE YOU RESIDE) SHOULD INCLUDE HEALTH CARE POWER of ATTORNEY, DESIGNATION of MEDICAL REPRESENTATIVE and DO-NOT-RESUSCITATE ORDER

INSURANCE and RETIREMENT

INSURANCE POLICIES & CONTRACTS
• LIFE
• LONG TERM
• DISABILITY
• PROPERTY

ACCOUNT & BENEFICIARY INFORMATION
• IRA
• ROTH IRA
• 401(k)

ANNUITIES
ANNUITY CONTRACTS

RELATION-SHIPS

MATRIMONY
MARRIAGE LICENSE

DIVORCE including "QUALIFIED DOMESTIC RELATIONS ORDER"

ADOPTION
ADOPTION PAPERWORK

IF I DIE or AM INCAPACITATED

important

A-Z

HAVE ALL YOUR NECESSARY DOCUMENTS IN ORDER & FILED?

KEY: ✓=HAVE IT   O= ACTION NEEDED   N/A= NOT APPLICABLE

Estate Planning

DOCUMENT	✓	O	N/A	LAST UPDATED
WILL / TRUST				
LETTER of INSTRUCTION w/				
list of: PEOPLE to CALL				
PERSONAL LETTERS to KIDS				
list of: ALL PASSWORDS				
COPY COPY of: BIRTH CERTIFICATE				
COPY COPY of: SOCIAL SEC. CARD				
COPY COPY of: CREDIT CARDS				

Proof of Ownership

DOCUMENT	✓	O	N/A	LAST UPDATED
DEED: REAL ESTATE				
DEED: LAND				
DEED: CEMETARY PLOT				
MORTGAGE INFORMATION				
PROOF OF: LOANS MADE				
PROOF OF: DEBTS OWED				
VEHICLE TITLE(S)				
BROKERAGE ACCT. INFO				
STOCK CERTIFICATES				
SAVINGS BONDS CERTS.				
OTHER INVESTMENTS				
BUSINESS OPERATING AGREEMTS.				
TAX DOCUMENTS (2-4YRS)				
other:				
other:				
other:				

Bank Accounts

DOCUMENT	✓	O	N/A	LAST UPDATED
list of: BANK ACCTS. + how TITLED				
list of: USERNAMES + PASSWDS.				
list of: SAFE DEPOSIT BOXES +KEYS				

Medical

DOCUMENT	✓	O	N/A	LAST UPDATED
PERSONAL HISTORY				
FAMILY HISTORY				
PET /VET INFO				
HIPPA FORMS				
LIVING WILL / AHCD				

Insurance & Retirement

DOCUMENT	✓	O	N/A	LAST UPDATED
POLICY: LIFE INSURANCE				
POLICY: LONG TERM INS.				
POLICY: DISABILITY INS.				
POLICY: PROPERTY INS.				
COPY COPY of: IRA ACCT + BENE. INFO				
COPY COPY of: ROTH IRA ACCT. + BENE.				
COPY COPY of: 401(k) / 403(b) INFO				
COPY COPY of: PENSION ACCT + BENE.				
ANNUITY CONTRACTS				
other:				

Relationships

DOCUMENT	✓	O	N/A	LAST UPDATED
MARRIAGE LICENSE				
DIVORCE INFORMATION				
ADOPTION PAPERWORK				

124

CHECKLIST

Protect Your Wild Places

✦ If you have a will or trust, find it, dust it off, and read it. Better yet, make a copy of it and use a highlighter to mark areas that either you don't understand or wish to change.

✦ If applicable, make an appointment with an attorney to update or create your estate plan.

✦ Create the image "How Do You Protect Yourself"—pg. 113

✦ Write about your image—pg. 114

✦ Call on your Protector Self—pg. 115

✦ Write a letter from your protector to yourself—pg. 116

✦ Take action on key messages your protector told you—pg. 117

✦ A History of Protection—pg. 118

✦ Reflect and deepen by writing about a specific memory—pg. 119

✦ Take Inventory of your insurance coverage and estate plan—pg. 120

✦ Create the image "In the Circle of Protection"—pg. 121

✦ Write and reflect on your new image—pg. 122

✦ Organize your files, using the chart "For the Record"—pg. 124

✦ **Breathe in deeply, and know that by doing this work you are expressing your love for the people in your life.**

VOCABULARY

IF YOU KNOW IT, CHECK IT OFF!
IF YOU DON'T, WRITE IN THE DEFINITION
FROM THE FIELD GUIDE!

- ☼ Term Life Insurance

- ☼ Permanent Life Insurance (bonus... can you name two types?)

- ☼ Disability Insurance (What is it, what does it do?)

- ☼ Long Term Care Insurance

- ☼ Umbrella Insurance

- ☼ Difference between a will and a trust

- ☼ Power of Attorney

- ☼ Advanced Directive for Healthcare (medical power of attorney)

- ☼ POLST

- ☼ Living Trust

- ☼ Irrevocable Trust

- ☼ Trustee vs executor

- ☼ Beneficiary

128

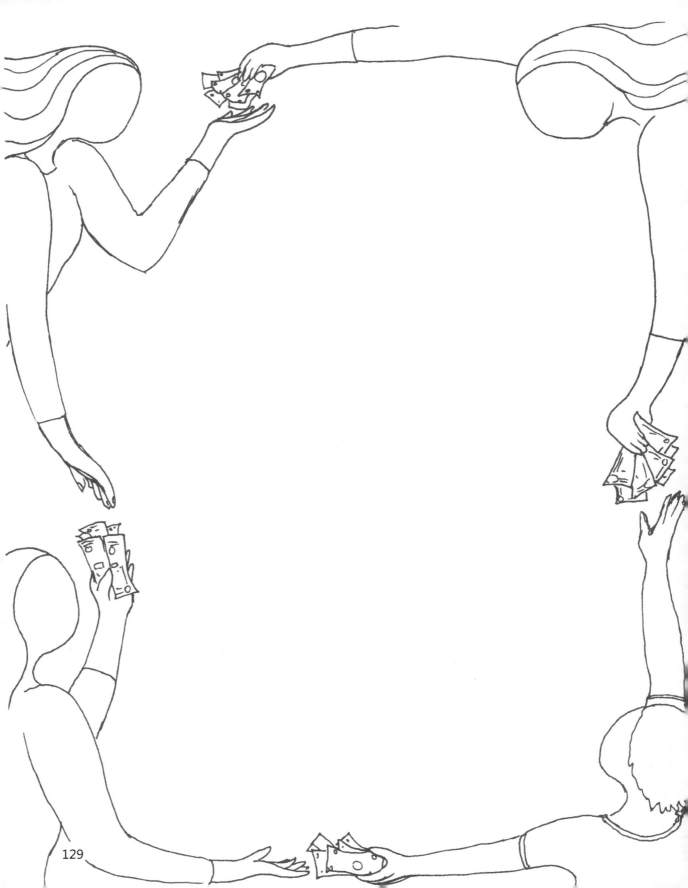

Chapter 7

GIVE WITH GUTS

CREATE

Your Relationship with Giving

Create or find an image that reflects your current relationship with giving. Do you give more than you can afford and put yourself at risk? Do you hesitate out of fear of scarcity? Is giving a source of joy or anxiety, confusion or celebration?

Title _____ Date _____

1 When it comes to giving I...

2 I find it difficult to give when...

3 An example of a time I gave time/money/stuff that I feel good about is...

4 When I give money to (family, people in need, non-profits), I...

5 When I feel best, I give...

6 What frustrates me about my giving is...

Historic Mind Map of Giving

Fill in this mind map, exploring the ways you experienced your family's generosity. If your parents or caregivers were very different to each other in this regard, consider doing separate maps for each of them. If you are uncertain of how to do a mind map, please refer to page 162.

Use a colored highlighter to mark the activities your parents did that you currently practice.

REFLECT

What do you see when looking at this mind map? What do you notice about where and how your parents/ caregivers gave of themselves? Are you like them? How are you different?

Write for five minutes starting with, "What I notice is..." or, "What strikes me about this mind map is..."

REFLECT

Receiving Generosity

Our desire and ability to be generous is colored, in part, by our experience of being the recipient of generosity. Think back on times when you were gifted money, unexpected gifts, opportunities, or someone's time.

Write any memories you have of receiving money, stuff, charity, or special treatment along with how you felt at the time.

Write for ten minutes about your reflections: Do you notice any themes? How has your experience of receiving another person's generosity impacted the way you give now?

Over-Giving

Write for five minutes about your own experience of over-giving, or of a time when you were the recipient of someone else's over-giving. What did you feel? How did you cope with your feelings?

What impact did your over-giving have on you and those around you? Ask your friends or family how they experienced your generosity, and see if you can start an honest dialogue about how your giving has impacted them.

Take the "no give" challenge. For a week, or better yet, a month, stop all giving as much as possible, especially if it involves any money leaving your pockets. Write everyday about what feelings come up, how your sense of self is impacted and what changes you might want to make in the future.

ACT

Stop. Start. Continue...

	PERSON/ORGANIZATION	TIME ⏱	MONEY $	STUFF 🎁	COMMENTS/NOTES
STOP					
START					
CONTINUE					

STOP. Who or what would you like to stop giving to?

START. Who or what would you like to give more to?

CONTINUE. Who or what are you currently giving to that you are happy with and want to continue? Don't forget things like caring for your mother, taking care of the neighbor's kids, tutoring a child, handling the fundraising for the football team.

CREATE!

The Future You

You've explored your roots and looked at your current practices regarding how you express generosity. What image comes to mind when you think of where you want to be in your relationship with giving? What illustrates your fullest, most graceful, sustainable, and healthy self?

Find or create an image of the person you are embodying when it comes to giving.

Title _____ *Date* _____

REFLECT

1 I love giving most when...

2 I now understand that, when it comes to giving...

3 The most important thing about giving is...

4 What I've learned about myself from exploring this is...

5 When I am in my most authentic self I give...

CHECKLIST

Give with Guts

⚙ Look back on the past year: how much money did you give away? What percentage of your annual income does it amount to? _____

⚙ Create the image "Your Relationship with Giving"—pg. 131

⚙ Reflect and write about this image—pg. 132

⚙ Complete Mind Map of Giving—pg. 133

⚙ Write about your insights—pg. 134

⚙ Reflect on Receiving Generosity—pg. 135

⚙ Complete the Over-Giving exercise—pg. 137

⚙ Fill in the Stop, Start, Continue chart—pg. 138

⚙ Create the image "The Future You"—pg. 139

⚙ Reflect on your image—pg. 140

⚙ **Set up an account or an envelope, and contribute a percentage of your income to it each month. Use this account whenever you do your giving.**

VOCABULARY

IF YOU KNOW IT, CHECK IT OFF!
IF YOU DON'T, WRITE IN THE DEFINITION
FROM THE FIELD GUIDE!

- ⚙ Charitable Deduction

- ⚙ Annual Gift Exemption

- ⚙ Donor Advised Fund

- ⚙ Annuity

- ⚙ Deferred vs. Immediate Annuity

- ⚙ Fixed vs. Variable Annuity

- ⚙ Real Estate Investment Trust (REIT)

- ⚙ Exchange Traded Fund (EFT)

- ⚙ Load vs. No Load

- ⚙ Socially Responsible Investing (SRI)

143

145

Chapter 8
TAKE YOUR WILD WITH YOU

Re-Evaluate Your Wild Strengths

	Wild Money Self Assessment		
1.	Right now I receive more than enough income to cover my personal expenses.	Yes	No
2.	I have a process for tracking or acknowledging the money I receive monthly.	Yes	No
3.	I feel grateful and excited about the money I receive each month.	Yes	No
4.	I understand the difference between my gross and net income.	Yes	No
5.	I express gratitude for the money that flows into my life.	Yes	No
6.	What I earn monthly is in alignment with the energy I put into the world.	Yes	No
7.	I know my Squeak-By number; what I need for basic expenses and minimum debt payments.	Yes	No
8.	I spend less than I make or receive each month.	Yes	No
9.	I feel good about the way I spend money.	Yes	No
10.	I know what my top five values are (what matters most to me), and my spending is in alignment with these values.	Yes	No
11.	I understand myself well enough to know how to avoid impulse spending.	Yes	No
12.	I pay attention to what I spend either by tracking in a check register, or by looking online every few days.	Yes	No
13.	I save at least 5% of my income monthly (into savings, retirement). (count this as a yes if you are retired)	Yes	No
14.	I know how much interest my savings are earning by percentage.	Yes	No
15.	When I use my savings for an emergency or large purchase, I replenish it as soon as possible.	Yes	No
16.	I understand my bank & brokerage statements and read them monthly.	Yes	No
17.	I can explain the difference between savings, money market and CDs.	Yes	No
18.	I have at least $5,000 in savings for emergencies or job loss.	Yes	No
19.	I can accurately define these words: stock, bond, mutual fund.	Yes	No
20.	I know the difference between dividends and interest	Yes	No
21.	I regularly invest my money (unless retired or on disability) and/or review what I am invested in.	Yes	No
22.	I understand my own risk tolerance/comfort zone when it comes to investing..	Yes	No
23.	I know myself well enough to either invest on my own or hire an advisor/planner.	Yes	No

24.	I know how a Roth IRA works and why it's a great vehicle for retirement savings (if you are retired, answer 'yes' to this question).	Yes	No
25.	I have good health insurance for myself and my family.	Yes	No
26.	If I have dependents (kids, parents, spouse), I have at least $250k in life insurance (if you have no dependents, answer "yes").	Yes	No
27.	I have either a living trust, or a will, power of attorney and advanced healthcare directive. (Estate plan)	Yes	No
28.	I understand how much insurance coverage I have for my home (renters or homeowners) and car(s), and know it's enough.	Yes	No
29.	Someone other than my spouse/partner knows where I keep my important documents, and if I have them in a safe, they know how to get in.	Yes	No
30.	I have reviewed my beneficiaries on retirement, annuities, and life insurance in the past two years.	Yes	No
31.	I have a regular practice of giving money or time to those in need.	Yes	No
32.	The amount of money/time I give away is in balance with what I have to give.	Yes	No
33.	I feel good about the way I practice generosity/philanthropy.	Yes	No
34.	I understand what motivates me to donate to a particular cause.	Yes	No
35.	I have a plan for how and to whom I give money.	Yes	No
36.	I have my charitable intent written into my estate plan (will or trust).	Yes	No

Now, for each section, give yourself one point for each yes, per category:

Purple (Receive):____   Red (Spend): ____   Yellow (Nurture): ____

Green (Grow): ____   Light Blue (Protect): ____   Indigo (Give): ____

Where you are now:

0 -10 points:	**Downright Domesticated**	—Time to get to work and mend your ways.
10-20 points:	**Wandering in the Woods**	—You are headed in the right direction.
20-30 points:	**Dancing with your Wild**	—You are doing great. Keep going.
30-36 points:	**Wondrous Wild Woman**	—Call me and teach me a thing or two!

On the next page, color the petals of the mandala. If you have six points in the blue section, fill in that petal completely; if you have only one point, fill in 1/6 of the petal.

Mandala Template

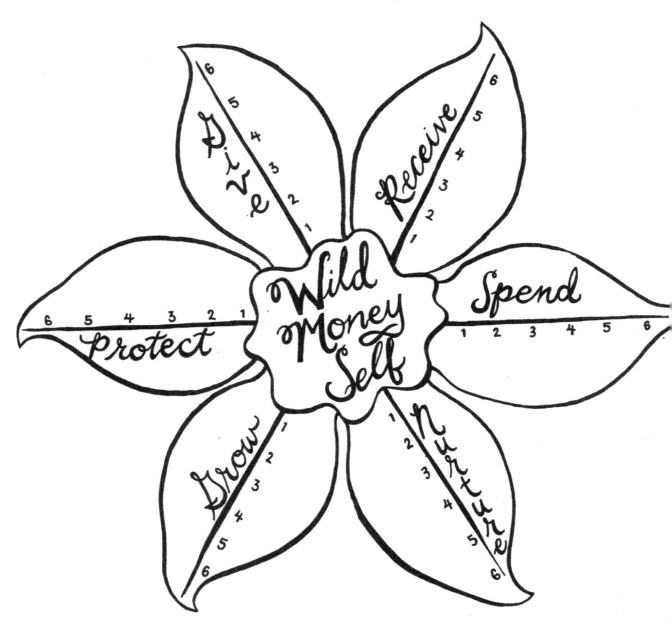

Compare your first mandala from page 13 with the mandala on the previous page. How have you grown?

Wild Money Retrospective

What you'll need:

- Color copies of all the images you created throughout this book
- A candle
- Soothing music
- Incense and /or fresh flowers
- An hour or two of uninterrupted time
- Scotch tape
- A camera (optional, but really fun!)
- Something comfortable to sit on

Arrange your drawings on the wall or floor according to the diagram on the next page. Your first image goes in the center.

WILD MONEY

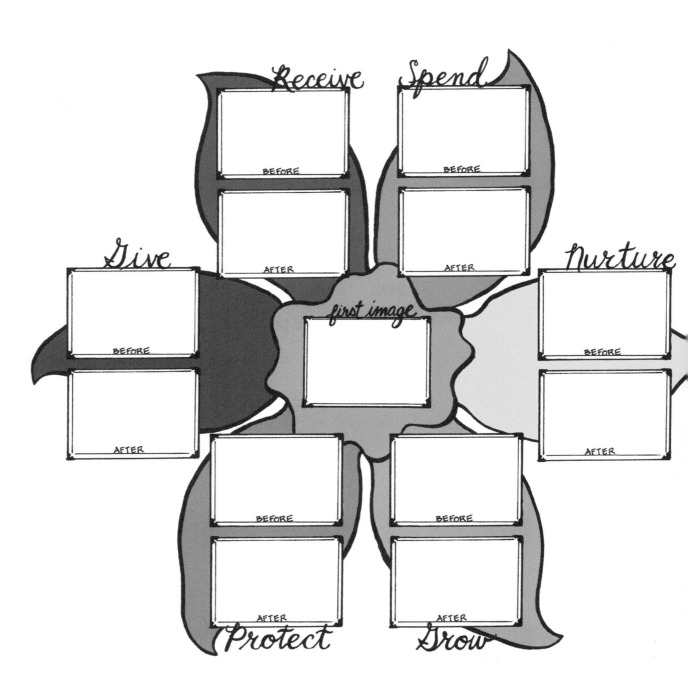

RETROSPECTIVE

OBSERVATIONS & FEELINGS

REFLECT

Retrospective Reflection

1 When I look at all my drawings/images, together, what I notice is...

2 It I had to name one central theme in my "before" images it would be.....

3 The central theme in my "after" pictures appears to be....

4 What I've learned about myself from this retrospective is....

5 What I've learned about my relationship to money is......

Write a Love Letter to Money

CREATE

Create a final image that represents the relationship with money you yearn for. Get specific. Dare to dream.

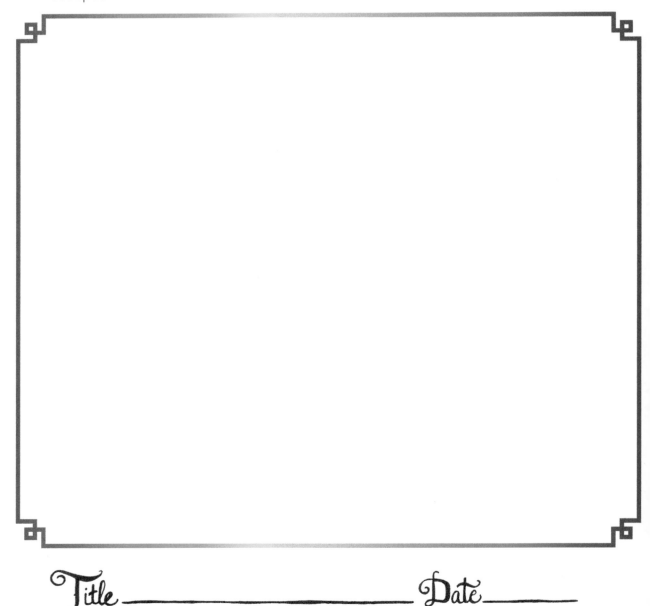

Title _____ Date _____

155

Make a list of 3-5 concrete, achieveable goals you want to commit to right now that will get you closer to your vision. Post them by your computer or in your planner.

Consider sharing your final image with a beloved friend or partner. Or make a small color copy of your image and carry it in your wallet or as a reminder of your new relationship with money.

Zelda's Wild Money
Completion Ritual

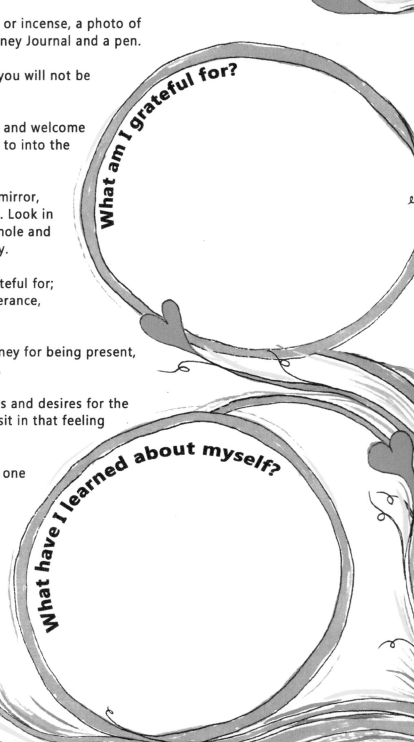

⚇ What you'll need: a candle, sage or incense, a photo of yourself, a mirror, your Wild Money Journal and a pen.

⚇ Choose a time and space where you will not be interrupted.

⚇ Light the candle and the incense and welcome yourself and whomever you pray to into the circle.

⚇ Place the photo of yourself, the mirror, and your journal near the candle. Look in the mirror and see yourself as whole and brave and competent with money.

⚇ Speak out loud what you are grateful for; appreciate your courage, perseverance, tenderness, and love.

⚇ Thank your relationship with money for being present, and taking this journey with you.

⚇ Share your prayers, wishes, hopes and desires for the future of your relationship. And sit in that feeling for a while, letting it sink in.

⚇ Close the circle by giving thanks one last time. Blow out the candle.

What am I grateful for?

What have I learned about myself?

What have I learned about money?

How have I been brave with money?

What I wish for myself!

Your photo here!

How to do a Mind Map

A mindmap helps you to brainstorm ideas in a visual way. Here are a few tips:

1. The center circle is the topic- such as "Emotions and Money"
2. Use lots of color to make it interesting, and to bring your attention to themes (for example: blue for positive feelings, red for negative feelings)
3. In the outlying circles put a word/image, and then free associate ideas that come from that word.

Here is an example from page 162. When doing a mind map to explore how your parents or care-givers expressed generosity you have several options, depending on the family you grew up in:

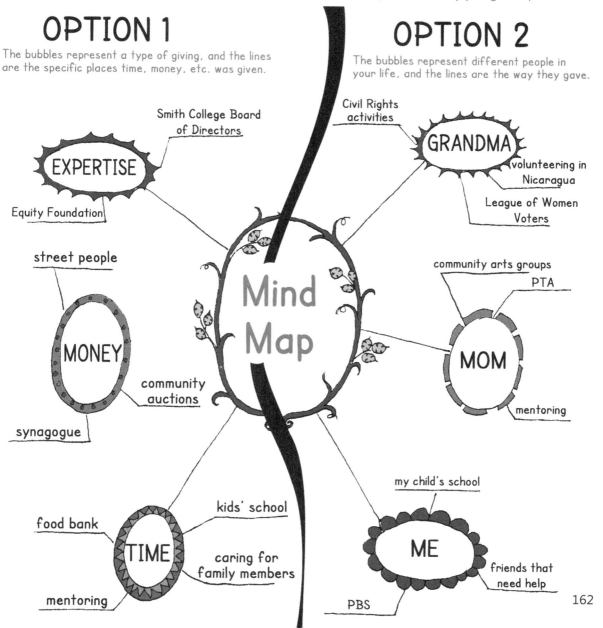

OPTION 1
The bubbles represent a type of giving, and the lines are the specific places time, money, etc. was given.

OPTION 2
The bubbles represent different people in your life, and the lines are the way they gave.

Smith College Board of Directors

EXPERTISE

Equity Foundation

street people

MONEY

synagogue

community auctions

Mind Map

Civil Rights activities

GRANDMA

volunteering in Nicaragua

League of Women Voters

community arts groups

PTA

MOM

mentoring

food bank

kids' school

TIME

caring for family members

mentoring

my child's school

ME

friends that need help

PBS

Musings * thoughts * diary * journal * chronicle * intentions * observations * scribbles * reflections *

Z GUIDE TO MONEY

A SASSY WOMAN'S FIELD GUIDE TO FINANCIAL TERMS

WILD MONEY

INVESTING

TERMS you should Know

INSURANCE

TAXATION

CONTENTS

Welcome to Zguide to Money. I called it Zguide because my name is Zelda! Of course! I'll be your guide through the wilderness of money; all those scary financial words and terms that have baffled you for years. I explain things using beauty and metaphor so that you will want to read this. What a concept, right?

If you're just getting curious about your finances, I hope this guide will whet your appetite for knowledge. If you already have investments--may this guide shine a little light onto terms you feel you "should" already know (but no one has yet helped you wrap your mind around them).

Either way, it's our hope that what you have in front of you will help you develop confidence and competence-- so the next time you meet with an advisor or talk with friends, you'll feel clued in and comfortable asking questions.

Wildly yours,

Zelda

Part I: Investing

Be an Owner and a Loaner

Investments can be divided into two categories: Ownership and Loanership. When you buy a stock, you become an owner of a tiny piece of that company's assets and earnings. In the image below, the stockholder would own a tiny piece of the cow, the machinery, the land and the milk. If the dairy does well, the value of your shares increases, but if it falters, you could potentially lose your investment. You buy stock—invest in a company—to grow your money, and in some cases, for the income (dividends) that you receive. As a shareholder, because you are an owner, the value of your investment fluctuates as the stock price changes.

BONDS =
LOANERSHIP

STOCKS =
OWNERSHIP

ONE SHARE

STOCK HOLDER

INVESTS MONEY

NOW "OWNS" A PIECE OF the ASSETS & EARNINGS

CEIVES EREST

LOANS MONEY

BOND HOLDER

DIVIDENDS

I vote yes!

MILK

CHEESE

166

Be an Owner With Stocks

Issuing stock is one way a company raises money. Publicly traded companies are ultimately accountable to their investors because as shareholders in the company they have a vote on important decisions like the election of the board of trustees.

Be a Loaner With Bonds

When you purchase a bond you are actually loaning your money in exchange for income. In the case illustrated on the previous page, the investor loans her money to the dairy so they can grow their business, and in exchange receives regular interest payments (thus bonds are referred to as "fixed" income). Buying a bond is generally safer than a stock because 1) you are not taking on the risk of ownership, 2) there is a promise to return your initial investment and 3) you receive a steady income from the interest the bond pays. You know it's a loan-type investment if it has a:

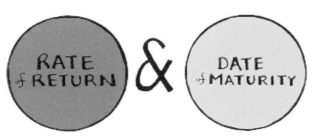

The interest that the bank, corporation or government is going to pay you for the privilege of using your money.

RATE of RETURN & DATE of MATURITY

How long you are agreeing to loan your money.

For example, if an ABC Natural Gas Bond pays 4% for 20 years then you know it's a loan type investment. Your expectation as the investor is that at the end of the term you are owed your original investment of $10,000, along with a steady fixed income for the duration of the bond.

"RATE of RETURN" = "YIELD" = "INTEREST RATE"
How much income you'll get in a given time
period for loaning your money

Stocks Pay Dividends

As a company becomes increasingly profitable, they may begin to pay dividends to their shareholders. A dividend is a sum of money paid regularly by a company to its shareholders out of its profits or reserves. Companies strive to continually increase their dividend payout as they grow, as this is often a sign of stability. The company decides what dividend to offer as a percentage of the share price. This percentage, shown as a dollar amount, is known as the dividend yield of the stock. The yield number fluctuates because it is tied to the price of the stock, which is always changing.

> *For example: ABC Corporation's Dividend= 5.6%, therefore its dividend yield is $3.70 based on a share price of $66.16.*

When you invest in dividend producing stocks, you have a choice of taking the dividends as cash income, or reinvesting them (buying more shares of stock).

This is like owning part of an apple tree. When the apples are picked, you get your share of the apples (your dividend). You can then choose to eat the apple (use the cash) or plant the apple seeds to grow more apple trees. Eventually, when the tree matures, you might decide to sell your shares of the tree—and because it's now bigger and produces wonderful fruit, you will get more per share than you paid. Likewise, if you try to sell your shares after a hurricane ripped off half its branches, you will get less than you initially invested.

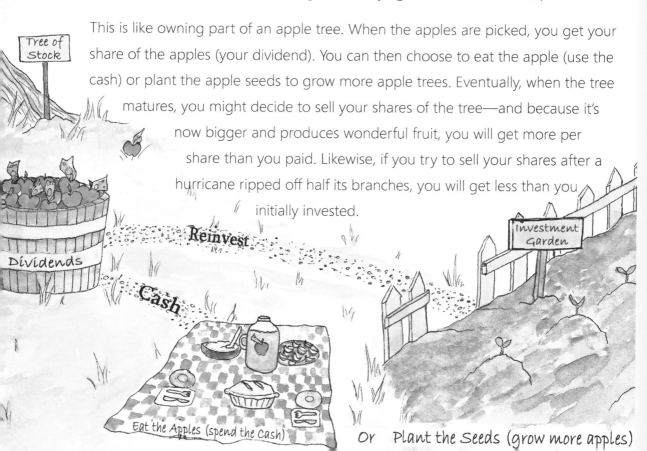

Tree of Stock

Dividends

Reinvest

Cash

Investment Garden

Eat the Apples (spend the Cash)   Or   Plant the Seeds (grow more apples)

Bonds Pay Interest

Interest is the payment you receive in exchange for loaning your money to a bank, municipality, government, or corporation. Just as you pay a mortgage company interest for using their money to purchase a house, as a bond holder, you typically want to get paid well for giving up your principal (the amount you invested) for a period of time.

It's important that you understand how bond interest will be taxed, as this can have a serious impact on your total return (interest-taxes=total return).

Certificates of Deposit (CDs)— issued by banks and usually have one to ten-year maturities.

- Best for short term savings (1-5 years)
- Interest is 100% taxable
- There are penalties for early withdrawal.

Corporate Bonds—issued by large corporations like Dupont, GE, IBM, Microsoft.

- Best used in retirement accounts, or for people with low to moderate incomes
- Interest is fully taxable – Federal, State, and Local
- Usually have the highest yields. Since corporate bond interest is taxable, they typically have to pay higher interest rates to appeal to investors.

Government Bonds—issued by the US government (Treasury bills, bonds, notes)

- Best for retirement accounts or people with moderate incomes
- Interest is taxable federally but is not subject to state or local taxes
- Typically have low yields because they are considered the safest investment (the lower the risk to the investor, the lower the yield)

The
COMPARATIVE TAXATION of BONDS

CERTIFICATE of DEPOSIT

CORPORATE BOND

GOVERNMENT BOND

MUNICIPAL BOND†

KEY

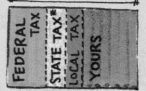

* YOUR STATE MAY NOT TAX

† USUALLY TAX FREE AS LONG AS YOU LIVE IN THE MUNICIPALITY WHERE IT WAS ISSUED.

Municipal Bonds—issued by state municipalities to raise money for projects like schools, airports, roads, and municipal services (also called Muni or tax-free bonds).

- Most appropriate for high income investors when used in taxable (non-retirement) accounts.
- Interest is federally tax-free to all, and state/local tax–free only when you live in the same state as where the bond was issued.
- Yields may be lower than corporate bonds because they are tax advantaged.

RECAP

OWNER/LOANER

Stock = Ownership Some stocks pay dividends (they never pay interest). You make money by the price of the shares increasing and by the dividend (if they pay one).

Bond = Loanership They have a RATE of return and a DATE of maturity. Bonds always pay interest with the intention of giving back your original investment when it matures.

Types of Owner/Loaner Investments

Stock	Bonds
Stock Mutual Fund	Bond Mutual Fund
Real Estate	Personally held
Precious Metals	contracts/mortgages
Business	CDs

How Risky is that Stock or Bond?

Bonds—The risk of a bond investment has to do with the credit-worthiness of the company or government issuing the bond. A bond issuer (usually a corporation, municipality or government) has a credit rating, like you have a credit score. If they want to improve this rating they can insure the investors' principal, which guarantees the investor that they will be paid back even if the bond issuer defaults. High yield bonds have to pay more interest because the investor takes more risk due to lower credit worthiness.

Types of Credit Worthiness in Bonds:

- *Investment Grade*—Higher credit rating, lower risk, typically lower interest rate
- *High Yield or Junk Bonds*—Lower credit rating, higher risk, higher interest rate

Stocks—The risk of a stock has to do with the company's size, stability, and industry.

- *Growth and Income:* Large companies that give a dividend of two percent or more. They are mature companies focused on stability and steady growth.
- *Growth:* Typically mid to large companies focused on growing. They tend to pour money into opening new markets, doing research and development, or improving their product line. If they give a dividend, it would be less than two percent.
- *Aggressive Growth:* Small to mid-sized companies, technology, or new companies. The smaller and more singularly focused the company, the more aggressive it is. There's more potential for growth, but the investor also assumes more risk.

Until you're wealthy enough to "retire" your money, It should be working as hard as possible—for you!

—Jerry Snavely

Asset Allocation

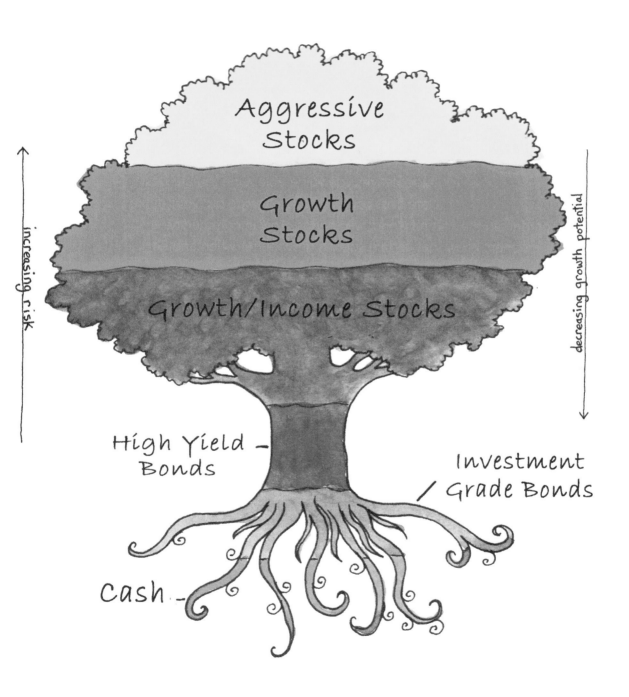

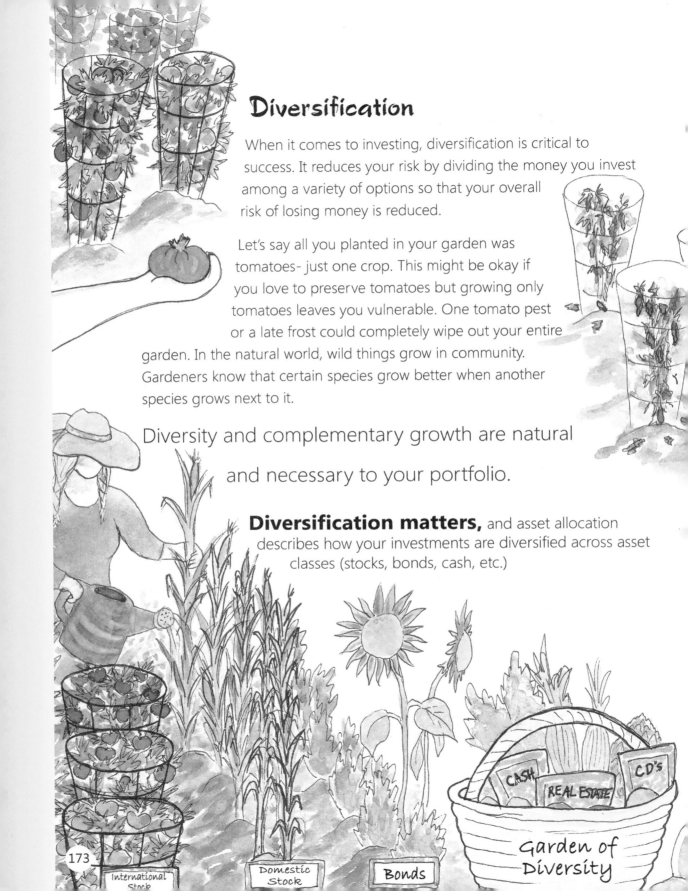

Diversification

When it comes to investing, diversification is critical to success. It reduces your risk by dividing the money you invest among a variety of options so that your overall risk of losing money is reduced.

Let's say all you planted in your garden was tomatoes- just one crop. This might be okay if you love to preserve tomatoes but growing only tomatoes leaves you vulnerable. One tomato pest or a late frost could completely wipe out your entire garden. In the natural world, wild things grow in community. Gardeners know that certain species grow better when another species grows next to it.

Diversity and complementary growth are natural and necessary to your portfolio.

Diversification matters, and asset allocation describes how your investments are diversified across asset classes (stocks, bonds, cash, etc.)

CASH

REAL ESTATE

CD's

Garden of Diversity

International Stock

Domestic Stock

Bonds

Ways to Diversify: Stock

Diversify by Company Size: Ever heard the term Large Cap or Small Cap? This refers to the capitalization of the company. Capitalization defines the size of the company as measured by the share price times the numbers of shares the company has authorized, issued, or sold to investors.

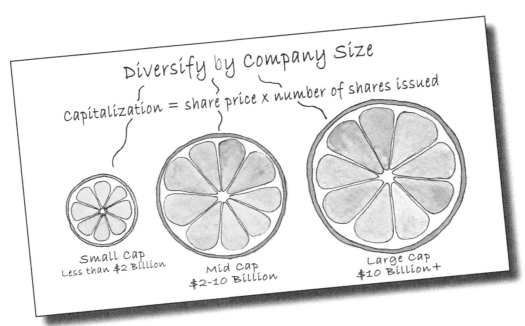

Small Cap = Highest risk (i.e. Earthlink, Constant Contact, Cracker Barrel, etc.)

Mid Cap= Medium risk (i.e. Best Buy, Delta Airlines, Dicks Sporting Goods, etc.)

Large Cap = Lowest risk (i.e. Microsoft, Intel, Target, Chevron, Walmart, etc.)

Example:

Orange Tech Company:

1 billion shares x $5 (current price) = capitalization is $5 Billion

The value of publically traded companies changes quickly these days because of the volatility of stock prices but roughly speaking, you can categorize stocks by their size.

Diversify by Country: Stocks can also be diversified by where the company is located.

Domestic - Companies headquartered in the United States (even if the majority of their revenue comes from overseas).

International - Companies headquartered outside the US.

Global - Refers to holdings in your portfolio (or in a mutual fund) that are both domestic and international.

Diversity by Industry: Generally speaking, you want to hold stocks from different industries and sectors of the economy such as energy, telecommunications, consumer goods, financial, real estate, and technology. This reduces the risk in a portfolio by spreading the investment over a broad spectrum of industries that will react differently to changing market conditions.

Ways to Diversify: Bonds

Diversify by Maturity Length: Since bonds all have a maturity date, you will have a more diverse and resilient portfolio by having bonds that mature at different times. For example, you may have two bonds maturing in five years, two in ten years, three in fifteen years, and three in twenty years. This is called a bond ladder. Thus, if you need the money, you know you have bonds maturing soon, and if you don't need the money when the bond matures, you can decide where to reinvest it. It is a huge disadvantage to have all your bonds mature at the same time because it means you will all-at-once have to find new bonds. If interest rates happen to be, as low as they are today, you would be stuck with very few options.

Diversify by Country: Bonds can be purchased from governments and companies around the world. The easiest way to add bonds from outside the US to your portfolio is through bond mutual funds. (More on this in the next section.)

30 years
Corporate Bond 5%

20 years
Airport Bond 3%

15 years
Corporate bond 4%

10 years
Hospital Bond 2.5%

5 years
US Treasury 1.2%

1 year

Bond Ladder

RECAP

ZELDA

DIVERSIFICATION

Diversification is about investing in many different investments as a way of lowering your risk.

With **STOCKS** you can diversify by:

❶ Company Size
small, mid, large

❷ Country
domestic, international, global

❸ Industry

With **BONDS** you can diversify by:

❶ Maturity Length

❷ Type
corporate, government, etc.

❸ Credit Rating

❹ Rate of Return

❺ Country of Issue

❻ Industry (if applicable)

Diversify by Industry: Just as one can buy stocks from a wide variety of companies from different industries, these same companies also issue bonds as a way to raise money for projects, expansion or growth. You could have bonds in your portfolio from a bank, an insurance company, an oil company, and a telecom company.

Diversify by Rate of Return: Wouldn't you always want the highest rate of return? Not always. Typically bonds that are maturing sooner will have lower interest rates and bonds with 20 or 30 year maturities will have higher interest rates. Essentially you are being rewarded for lending your money longer. You have to balance how much interest is being paid with how long you are committing your money to a particular bond.

Diversity by Credit Rating: Bonds have credit ratings, just like you and I have a credit score. Typically, the higher the company's credit rating, the lower the interest rate offered. Why? Because a higher credit rating means you are taking less risk, so they don't have to pay higher interest to entice customers to buy their bonds. People want safe investments and are willing to get paid a little less in exchange for safety.

Mutual Funds

A mutual fund is a portfolio of stocks or bonds or a combination of both, managed by a professional, with a particular objective such as "International Small Company Fund" or "Large Cap Growth Fund."

You can invest directly into a mutual fund by buying shares through a broker or online, or you can invest indirectly by investing through pension plans, insurance products, retirement accounts, and managed money programs. Many people own mutual funds and don't even know it.

Let me explain mutual funds using food as an analogy. If I want dinner, I can: 1) cook it myself; 2) hire a personal chef; or 3) go out to dinner. If I'm too busy to cook it myself, and hiring a personal chef isn't in my budget, I'm going to go out to eat. If I had cooked at home, I still would have spent money on ingredients, but not on labor or operations, right? At a restaurant, I'll potentially (but not always) pay more to have the food prepared and dishes done. I'm also paying for the chef, for the quality of the food they use, for the location of the restaurant, and the ambience.

In this scenario, dinner represents your investments. Stocks, bonds, and cash are the ingredients in your investment "dinner". You can go to the market and hand pick your investments. You do the research, make the individual trades, and watch for opportunities. In essence, you can be the cook. Or, you can invest in a mutual fund where someone else does the cooking. That mutual fund, just like a restaurant, decides the menu: its focus or objective.

The objectives answers these questions:

○ Which types of investments will be in the fund? For instance, will the mutual fund hold large cap international stocks or small cap domestic stocks?
○ Who is going to be the **portfolio manager**—the chef who decides on the best ingredients for the desired result or performance?
○ How much will it cost to participate in the fund? The expenses of running a fund are passed on to the investor and may range from .30% to over 2.0%

The mutual fund's **prospectus** (a lengthy, boring document full of legal disclosures and a few important details, that you receive when purchasing a mutual fund) obligates the fund to stick to what they said they would do. The mutual fund managers determine the fund's objective, just as the chef decides what's on the menu. This is to prevent a situation where investors think they have a diversified portfolio, but in reality, don't. You choose the fund, like you would choose a restaurant, but the fund managers choose the individual stocks and bonds.

Chef Portfolio Manager

Mutual Funds Reduce Risk
by Increasing Diversification

Stock

Mutual Fund

More Risk

Greater Support

How Risky is that Mutual Fund?

A mutual fund typically holds over a hundred stocks if it is purely a stock fund. If bonds are included, they often hold hundreds of individually issued bonds. More individual stocks and bonds mean you have greater diversity and less risk.

Look at the image of the woman on the swing. Which swing would you prefer to ride on, the one with a single rope or the one with multiple ropes? If the single rope broke, the swing would crash to the ground just as your investment would diminish if the stock failed to perform. With a mutual fund, the failure of one company will not bring the whole fund down; thus, you are taking less risk by spreading your investment over a diversified portfolio. You could gamble on a single stock and hope it hits a home run—like Apple has for the past few years—but that is a risk to take with money you aren't counting on for the future. Building your retirement accounts and emergency savings are the first priority, You can have some fun on the single-rope swing if you don't have too far to fall, but it's not for the faint of heart.

Mutual funds aren't risk-free, and some mutual funds are riskier than others depending on which types of investments they are focused on. A large cap stock fund is less aggressive than a small cap stock fund. *You still need to pay attention to what kind of mutual fund you are buying relative to your own comfort zone and risk tolerance.*

What it Costs to Own a Mutual Fund

It's true, it costs money to make money. One of the keys to investing wisely, is to understand what it costs you and to be able to analyze the value you get for the money spent. This is called Return on Investment or ROI.

> **Expenses and Fees:** Look in the fund's prospectus to find out how much of the profit is retained by the mutual fund company to pay expenses for portfolio managers, administration, trading, and marketing. This can vary widely from .25% to over 2.5%. Typically, performance numbers on mutual funds are "net" of these fees, meaning that the cost of running the fund is deducted before they report how well the fund has done.

Load vs. No Load: The word "load" refers to a sales charge or commission that compensates a financial professional for selling and servicing the mutual fund. With a loaded fund, an advisor helps you choose which funds to use, provides planning services, handles the paperwork, and hopefully stays in touch with you throughout the years.

A no-load fund is one that is sold directly to you, the investor, and means there is no sales charge, and no advice given. To buy a no-load mutual fund, you go online and make the fund choice yourself. Another option to buying a loaded fund is to hire a professional by the hour to advise you on no-load fund choices, and then you do the buying and selling yourself. If you have a large

portfolio of funds, you might hire someone to manage it for an annual fee. It all depends on what you are most comfortable with and what you have time for.

How Loaded Funds Work:

Loaded funds come in three flavors, creatively named: A, B, or C shares. Which one you choose has to do with:

      1) The amount of money you are investing
      2) How long you plan to have your money in the mutual fund
      3) The preference/bias of your advisor

Think of it like this: If you need a car, you can choose to rent, lease or buy, right? You would make the decision about which of these makes sense based on how long you need a car and how much money you have.

- **C shares** are like renting a car: "C" share (constant load) is best for short term (one to five years) and less than fifty thousand dollars. The advisor is paid 1% per year, by the mutual fund company, for investing and managing your money.

- **B shares** are like leasing car: "B" share (back-end load) might be best with less than fifty thousand dollars to invest, but more time to let the investment grow. You do not pay to get into the fund, but are charged if you sell out of it before seven years has passed. This is also called a "Contingent Deferred Sales Charge" or CDSC.

- **A shares** are like owning a car: "A" share (front end load) is best if you have more than fifty thousand dollars in one mutual fund family. The load or sales charge is paid when you first invest (at the front end) because you get a discount on the percent charged, the more money you invest. This is called a breakpoint—you get a price break at different points: $50k, $100k, $250k, $500k, etc. Each time you hit that point by adding more money, or by your investment growing to that amount, you will receive a reduced sales charge for any new money invested in the same mutual fund.

WHAT CLASS SHARE DO I OWN?

ON YOUR BROKERAGE STMT...

ABC FUND **CLASS A**
XYZ BOND FUND **CLASS C**

RECAP

ZELDA
MUTUAL FUND

A MUTUAL FUND is a portfolio of stocks and/or bonds that has ❶ A portfolio manager ❷ An objective outlined in the prospectus and ❸ Expenses that are charged for participating. You can buy them yourself in NO-LOAD funds or through an advisor in LOADED funds.

⊢ADVANTAGES⊣

❶ DIVERSIFICATION
Even with a small amount of money, you can invest in a wide range of securities.
❷ CONVENIENCE
Funds are easily bought, sold and exchanged.
❸ PROFESSIONAL MANAGEMENT
❹ MINIMAL INITIAL INVESTMENT
For most funds this is between $1000 and $2500, or if you commit to a regular monthly contribution. (called DOLLAR COST AVERAGEING) You can invest as little as $50 a month in many funds.

⊢DISADVANTAGES⊣

❶ DIVERSIFICATION "PENALTY"
Diversification helps to reduce risk, but also limits your potential for a "home run" in an individual stock.
❷ NO GUARANTEES
You are investing in the market and taking risk along with it.
❸ COSTS
In some cases the cost of owning a fund outweighs its performance when considering loads and fees. Evaluate a fund by looking at "net" returns-the trun return after all costs are deducted.

Exchange-Traded Funds (ETFs)

ETF funds are ten or more stocks or bonds traded as a unit. Unlike mutual funds, which are bought or sold after the market closes each day, ETFs are "exchange traded"—meaning they are bought and sold in "real time" (when financial markets are open and trading). They are best for situations in which you want more exposure to a sector of the market without the risk of owning only one stock. *Think of it like this:* If you want to own alternative energy investments, you could buy one or two individual stocks, or you could buy an ETF made up of twenty or thirty alternative energy companies. This way you have a broader exposure to the sector and have lowered your risk.

ETFs have lower expenses than mutual funds and they trade like a stock so you have more control over the price when buying or selling your shares. Often ETFs allow you to get exposure to markets that individual investors cannot access. For example, you could buy a Korean or Israeli ETF that holds the top 20 companies from each country. It would be difficult for you, as a small investor, to hold these 20 stocks individually, so the ETF allows me to make one trade and gives you less risk for exposure to specific markets.

RECAP

ETFs

EFTs are portfolios of stocks, bonds or both that trade like a stock. They provide diversity, liquidity, low cost to participate and some degree of professional management.

Real Estate Investing

Real estate is an important way to diversify your portfolio. For most people, owning a home is the first, important step. Then you can consider other ways to invest in real estate. You can buy a property yourself and manage it (or hire it out). If you buy when prices are low, and make more money from rent than it costs to own (paying the mortgage, taxes, insurance, and saving for repairs/vacancies), then you have a positive cash flow property. With real estate you control what

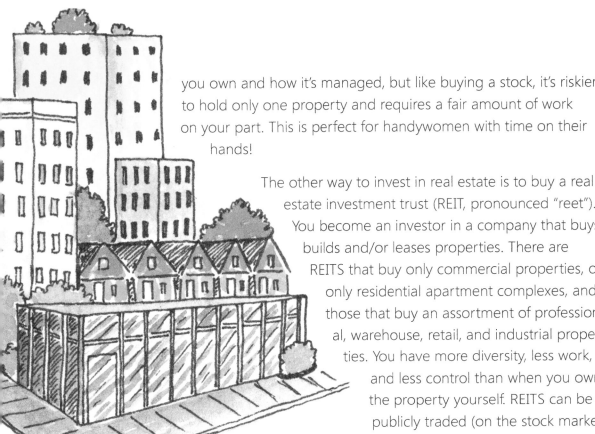

you own and how it's managed, but like buying a stock, it's riskier to hold only one property and requires a fair amount of work on your part. This is perfect for handywomen with time on their hands!

The other way to invest in real estate is to buy a real estate investment trust (REIT, pronounced "reet"). You become an investor in a company that buys, builds and/or leases properties. There are REITS that buy only commercial properties, or only residential apartment complexes, and those that buy an assortment of profession-al, warehouse, retail, and industrial proper-ties. You have more diversity, less work, and less control than when you own the property yourself. REITS can be publicly traded (on the stock market) or privately held. With a privately held REIT you purchase shares di-rectly with the REIT, can only sell your holdings at the end of the term (usually five to seven years) and need to have a larger initial investment.

You can buy REAL ESTATE by:
1. Owning properties yourself
2. Buying REITs that trade on the stock market
3. Buying privately traded REITs
4. Buying real estate ETFs
5. Buying real estate mutual funds
6. Buying mutual funds that own REITs along with many other well diversified stocks.

Whew! So many options!

Annuities

An annuity is an investment with an insurance wrapper. Like having a safety net under a roller coaster, buying an annuity lessens your risk through insuring your investment. **The purpose of all annuities is to provide a stable long-term income stream, either for life or for a fixed period of time.**

When you invest money directly, you're taking on the risk your money will grow and provide you with reliable income in retirement. When you buy an annuity from an insurance company, that company takes on the risk and guarantees you regular payments for life or for a fixed period of time. As the investor, you're able to transfer both the investment risk and the risk of living so long that you run out of money to the insurance company — so make sure the insurance company is well rated!**

** For information on how annuity companies are rated go to www.weissratings.com

The challenge in understanding annuities is that there are many different annuity products on the market, all with unique benefits. It can be confusing, but if you grasp the basic elements, you'll be more prepared to ask questions. **Remember, there are no dumb questions!**

Originally annuities were created as a retirement vehicle for people that didn't have access to company pensions. You can fund an annuity with a lump sum, or in regular payments, just like contributing to a 401k. Annuities are tax-deferred (no taxes are paid on the growth of the investment until you withdrawal the money) and have the ability to guarantee an income stream, which can add some security and stability to retirement cash flow.

Types of Annuities

Annuities can be *immediate* (you invest your money and begin to receive payments immediately), or *deferred* (payments are deferred until you need the money at a later date).

Immediate Annuity
You receive regular payments as soon as you invest: you can "eat it immediately."

Deferred Annuity
You wait to receive payments, thus the investment "matures and bears fruit."

safety net

Fixed Annuity

Has a fixed interest rate and a date of maturity, thus returns are "fixed."

Variable Annuity (VA)

Has portfolio of funds you choose, with a safety net for protection-thus, returns are "variable."

The two most common types of annuities are **fixed** and **variable**, which refers to the underlying investments used in the product. A fixed annuity has a guaranteed rate of return for a period of time, like a bond, except that it's an insurance contract that can provide a stream of income for a fixed period of time. Variable annuities offer the investor the opportunity to invest in a portfolio of subaccounts, like mutual funds, and offer a guaranteed death benefit and income stream.

Annuities have the following features:

1) Tax Deferred—you don't pay any tax on the interest, dividends, or growth in the annuity until you withdraw the money.

2) Death Benefit—all annuities have a death benefit that may be more or less than the actual current value of the investment.

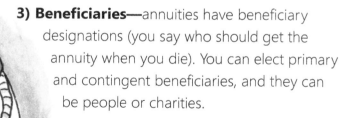

3) Beneficiaries—annuities have beneficiary designations (you say who should get the annuity when you die). You can elect primary and contingent beneficiaries, and they can be people or charities.

Note: beneficiaries designated in an annuity, life insurance, or retirement plan supersede anything you may write in a will or trust.

4) Guarantees—As an insurance product, annuities offer a variety of guarantees depending on the product. For example, it may guarantee income for life, a certain rate of return, or a death benefit that increases by 5% per year. You may have come across the phrase "subject to the claims paying ability of the insurance company." Guarantees are only as good as the guarantor (the insurance company).

5) Tax Free Exchanges—You can move from one annuity to another without tax consequences (called a 1035 exchange). Tax is due on the gain in the annuity only when you take distributions (withdrawals).

Just as you pay to get insurance coverage on your home or car, the insurance component of an annuity has a cost (internal fees and commissions) that needs to be considered alongside the benefits when deciding whether or not purchase one.

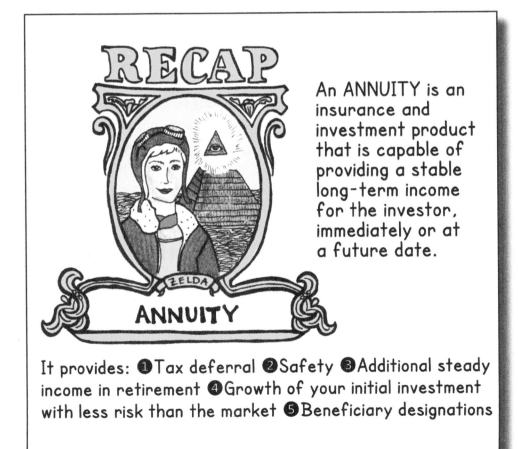

An ANNUITY is an insurance and investment product that is capable of providing a stable long-term income for the investor, immediately or at a future date.

It provides: ❶Tax deferral ❷Safety ❸Additional steady income in retirement ❹Growth of your initial investment with less risk than the market ❺Beneficiary designations

Socially Responsible Investing (SRI)

Although SRI is not a type of investment, it describes a manner of investing that is worth discussing. SRI integrates investing for financial gain with doing good, and supports companies that are actively working to be better global citizens. Call it green, ethical, or socially responsible, SRI is about investment decision making that is integrated with personal values.

SRI investors are concerned about global issues such as poverty, pollution, climate change, human rights, corporate behavior, and the environment. During the past thirty years, the sustainable investment industry has grown exponentially both in the number of investors participating, and in the impact on and clout it has with the corporate world.

Initially investors were focused on a **"Do No Harm"** approach in which they avoided companies that were environmentally negligent or that produced harmful products, like tobacco. In the second phase of the SRI growth cycle, **"Doing Well by Doing Good"** described how many companies worked to reduce costs and enhance profits through pollution prevention, waste minimization, energy efficiency, and other relatively simple business strategies. Now, in phase three, **"Sustainability"** is becoming central to how businesses are run. Green practices drive growth by encouraging innovation, reducing environmental impact, increasing sales and offering competitive advantage."

How SRI mutual funds work:

Publically traded companies are evaluated using social screens such as corporate governance, diversity, human rights, product safety, and indigenous rights. If a company passes through this screening process, then the portfolio manager can consider adding it to the portfolio, assuming the company is financially solid, and fits the objective of the fund. When a company's social policies change for the worse the portfolio manager may choose to boot them out of the fund.

As a socially responsible investor you can buy socially screened mutual funds, ETF's, or, with larger portfolios, you can participate in privately managed portfolios. You can also do your own research and create a personal stock portfolio that you build according to your own social criteria.

How SRI Funds Work

Publically traded stocks in U.S. 8,700

Social Screens
* environmental
* human rights
* diversity
* health & safety

Portfolio Manager

investors

Social Researcher

Stocks that pass social screens

Financial

SRI portfolio

GREEN FD

There are a wide range of social screens used within the SRI mutual fund community. Some funds focus on the environment, others promote women's issues, or a particular set of religious values. Mutual Funds can define SRI a number of different ways. It's important to understand the fund's selection criteria and why certain companies make the cut. For example, a company like GE or Apple might be included in one SRI portfolio but not another because the funds have different criteria. One fund may promote SRI by holding stock of a less responsible company in order to be a shareholder and pressure the corporation to change their labor practices. Another fund might make a statement about social responsibility by excluding that stock from their holdings..

A common misconception is that if you make the choice to invest in SRI funds, you will sacrifice performance. This has not tended to be true; perhaps in part because the screening itself tends to weed out companies with shady business practices. Take the time to compare funds that are similar in nature, and look at their long-term track records (at least three years, but five or ten is better). Remember that you may choose to invest one hundred percent of your portfolio in SRI funds, or create a hybrid portfolio of traditional and socially screened investments.

RECAP

ZELDA

SRI

SRI stands for socially responsible investing. SRI involves multiple levels of screening of companies for social issues like: human/animal rights, environmental, product safety, and corporate governance. Additionally, SRI investors collaborate on share holder resolutions which seek to improve corporate behavior and practices.

PART II: Taxation of Accounts

Now that you've learned about the types of investments available, let's look at the different buckets—account types—that you can put investments into.

Why buckets? Because a bucket, like an account, is a container. Within the account, you can hold many different types of investments—stocks, bonds, CDs, annuities, mutual funds, and cash/money market funds. In other words, you have a pond of possible investments, and the choice you make when buying an investment, is what kind of account you want to hold it in. You can choose between three different buckets, or account types, that determine the tax treatment of the money within the account:

1 Taxable (investment accounts)

2 Tax Deferred (retirement plans, pensions, annuities)

3 Tax Deferred and Tax Free (Roth IRA and Roth 401k)

Taxable

Investment Account

**Tax-Deferred
(100% taxable)**

Traditional
IRA
SEP
SIMPLE

**Tax-Deferred
(100% tax free)**

Roth
IRA

194

Taxable: These are your non-retirement accounts, bank accounts, or the stock portfolio you inherited from Aunt Edith. Taxable really means that the income (dividends, interest, or capital gain) on these accounts is taxed each year as it occurs, even if you reinvest the dividends on your stock or mutual fund. Basically, anything that is not a retirement account is a taxable account although, within that account, you may have individual investments that are tax free, like municipal bonds, or tax deferred, like annuities.

Tax Deferred: Tax deferred simply means you'll pay taxes eventually, but in the meantime you don't have to pay as it grows, nor do you have to worry about capital gains* incurred from selling an asset with the account. In a retirement account (401k, 403b, traditional IRA, SEP IRA, etc.) you are putting money in that has not yet been taxed (pre-tax or deductible from current income), so that everything in the account has a big fat IOU to the IRS on it. When you take distributions from a retirement account (after age 59 ½) you will owe taxes on the amount you take out, and the withdrawal will be added to your income.

In most cases, if you take the money out before 59 ½, you'll pay a whopping ten percent penalty on top of the taxes. Ouch!

Tax Deferred and Tax Free: There are only two ways to escape taxation in this country, legally—put money in a Roth IRA or Roth 401k every year, or buy municipal bonds. Since here we are discussing account types, we are only going to discuss Roths.

*defined on page 210

RECAP

TAXATION

There are 3 types of accounts you can use for your investments:

1 TAXABLE ACCOUNTS
You pay taxes on income and gains each year.

2 TAX DEFERRED
A. 100% TAXABLE retirement accounts (traditional IRA, 401k, pensions)
B. 100% TAX FREE retirement accounts when the money is withdrawn after the age of 59½ (ROTH)

A Roth IRA or Roth 401k is funded (you put money into it) with after-tax money—either you've paid income tax on it, or it was gift. As long as you keep the earnings in the Roth until you are 59 ½ or older, all that this account has earned is yours to use tax free. You can also pass it to your beneficiaries and they won't pay taxes either. A little known fact about Roth IRA's is that the principal (what you originally contributed) is always yours to use should you need it without taxes or penalty. I'm not recommending you strip the money out of your Roth, but because you funded it with after-tax money, the IRS can only put limits and penalties on the growth in the account, not the principal. Nice to know!

Remember!

All investments (stocks, bonds, mutual funds, CDs, cash, annuities) can be held in any of the accounts named above unless limited by the provider (as in a 401k).

PART III: Insurance

I know that for many of you insurance feels like a luxury or fantasy, especially health insurance. But this is really important.

Think about it, auto insurance is the law in most states, so few of us go without it. Mortgage companies require homeowners insurance to protect their investment, so most people have that as well.

If you rent your home or apartment, please get renter's insurance—it's very affordable. And do whatever you can to get health insurance. These come before any of the insurance listed here.

If you're covered on home and health—read on!

If you don't have them-go to page 215 for resources—right now!

Wildly Yours,

Zelda

Understand Life Insurance

At its most basic, life insurance is a promise made by an insurance company to give a beneficiary a tax free, lump sum of money (death benefit) should the insured person die.

An insurance agent or financial planner can help you determine how to set up life insurance so that it provides the control, tax protection and benefit that you are looking for.

Term life Insurance is like renting a house; as long as you pay the rent (premium), you have a place to live. In this case, you are granted the right to the death benefit for a term, between one and thirty years, and after the term ends, the insurance benefit goes away. The easiest way to remember this is to think of it as temporary insurance—and for that reason it is used for temporary needs, like taking care of children, or paying for their education should you die prematurely. Term insurance is much more affordable than permanent insurance because you have no equity (or cash value) in the policy.

Note: Most of the life insurance offered through an employer is term insurance; your term is your employment rather than a set number of years. Leave the job and the insurance ends. It is advisable to have at least some of your life insurance outside of work so that you don't lose all coverage when a job terminates.

Permanent life insurance is like buying a house—as long as you pay your mortgage, you will always have a place to live, and you are building equity in the house. In other words, with permanent life insurance, you can't outlive the policy in most cases. When premiums are paid on a permanent policy, part of the money pays for the insurance and part goes toward the cash value (that is invested), and builds equity in the policy. You can get access to that equity by borrowing or withdrawing it in the future. Permanent insurance can be used to protect a dependent spouse or child, transfer wealth from one generation to the next, protect business partners, and/or as an investment vehicle.

There are two basic types of permanent life insurance: **Whole Life** and **Universal Life.**

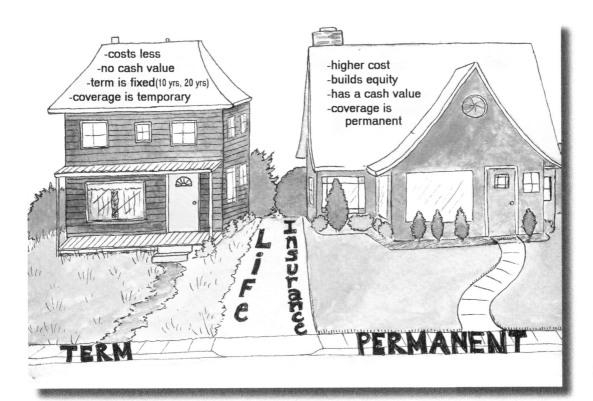

Whole Life Insurance, as its name implies, provides coverage for your whole life rather than a set number of years like term insurance. Premiums are typically paid monthly or annually at the same rate for your entire lifetime. Part of your premium is credited to the cash value of the policy. You can access the cash value during your lifetime through a guaranteed loan from the insurance company. Whole Life insurance is generally more expensive and less flexible than Universal Life but provides the highest level of guarantees of all permanent life insurance products.

Universal Life Insurance(UL) also provides coverage for your entire life, yet has greater flexibility than Whole Life. The policy is flexible because you can pay premiums for your whole life, for a limited number of years, or in a lump sum. You can also adjust the death benefit of the policy (within company guidelines) as your circumstances change. The policy can be structured to provide high cash value accumulation, guaranteed death benefits, or a combination of each. You can buy a UL policy that allows you to invest the cash value in stocks and bonds (called mutual fund sub-accounts), where you take the risk of how well the investments perform—This is called Variable Universal Life, because the cash value varies with stock market fluctuations. There are also policies that guarantee the rate of return, putting the risk on the insurance company—providing less risk and more safety. As with all investments and insurance products, determining the right one for you is critical, and should be based on your long term needs and tolerance for risk.

RECAP

LIFE INSURANCE comes in two genres: TERM and PERMANENT. TERM insurance is cheaper, has a fixed term, and NO CASH VALUE. PERMANENT insurance will last a lifetime, builds cash value (so you have equity in the policy) and is significantly more expensive—yet in the long run, because it never goes away, may be a better investment. PERMANENT life insurance has two categories: WHOLE LIFE and UNIVERSAL LIFE.

LIFE INSURANCE

Disability Insurance

Most insurance protects your nest eggs; assets like your home, car, health, or business. What about protecting the goose that created the eggs in the first place? Your income is your greatest asset and if you are still earning that income, it might make sense to insure it. This is where disability insurance comes in. It protects a portion of your income if you become partially or fully disabled. Typically, a long term disability policy will replace up to sixty percent of your current income, and goes into effect after an elimination period (much like the deductible on your car insurance) of 30, 60, 90, or 180 days. The benefit may last two or five years, or until you reach age 65. Many policies offer inflation protection so that the benefit amount increases every year by three to five percent.

To qualify for a disability claim, you have to meet three criteria: 1) Be sick or injured 2) Be under a doctor's care and 3) Suffer a twenty percent loss of time from work duties.

Getting disability insurance independently can be tricky, though it's worth exploring. Insurance companies will typically not cover people who work from home more than sixty percent of the time, and are biased against mental health treatment, chiropractic treatment, and progressive long-term health issues. That said, especially if you are the sole provider for your family, protecting your income stream is vitally important to explore.

Many employers offer both short and long-term group disability policies, and they are often worth investing in as long as you are first funding your retirement, have savings, and have little-to-no consumer debt. In other words, disability insurance can be a very important part of your financial plan, but it comes after the other pieces are established and funded.

DISABILITY INSURANCE replaces a percentage of your income if you lose the ability to perform your job. You can buy it through work or independently.

Three things must be true to claim on a policy:
1. You've suffered a 20% loss of time from work.
2. You're seeing a doctor.
3. You're sick or injured.

It is a valuable tool, once other financial priorities are in place.

Long Term Care Insurance

This is a hot topic these days as boomers retire, get ill, and fill up retirement homes and facilities around the country. Long term care (LTC) insurance protects your assets and income from being diverted to pay for the cost of long-term custodial care. It does not cover medical or acute care—that's what your health insurance is for—but it pays for care and support for a person who is no longer able to do things for herself. Most policies now cover home care, group or foster care, and assisted/nursing care in a facility.

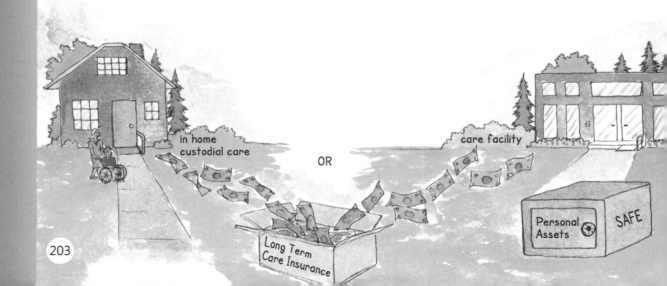

How does it work? There are four components to any LTC policy: 1) Daily/monthly benefit amount, 2) Duration of the benefit, 3) Inflation protection and 4) Elimination period. When an insurance company quotes how much a policy will cost, they look at your age and health history—these are the givens. Then, you choose the components based on what you can afford to pay and what will give you the most peace of mind.

In other words, a policy with a $4,000 monthly benefit that starts paying out after a 90-day elimination period, and lasts for three years with five percent inflation protection, will cost less than the same policy that last five years. Each of these components can be changed allowing you the capacity to build a policy that meets your needs and your budget.

To qualify to receive a long term care benefit, you must be unable to perform two out of six "activities of daily living," or ADLs: eating, toileting, continence, transferring, bathing, and dressing. And although most of us think of LTC insurance as only for the elderly, if you were in a car accident, or developed multiple sclerosis at the age of 50, you might qualify for benefits. Like disability insurance, this is an important consideration after you have the other building blocks in place.

RECAP

LTC INSURANCE

LONG TERM CARE insurance is not medical insurance—it covers custodial care at home or in a facility. It protects your assets from being spent down. The policy cost is based on several factors:

1. Age at purchase
2. Health
3. Benefit amount and duration
4. Elimination period
5. Whether or not inflation protection is included

Umbrella Insurance

This is liability insurance that is added to your primary car and homeowner's policies. It is called umbrella insurance because it protects your assets more broadly than your primary coverage does. Since this policy is designed to cover liability claims over and above what you have on your auto and home policies, it effectively increases the liability limits on both. Umbrella insurance is relatively inexpensive and can only be purchased through your home and auto insurer.

For example, if you carry an auto insurance policy with liability limits of $500,000, and a home-owners insurance policy with a limit of $300,000 then, with a million dollar umbrella, your limits effectively become $1,500,000 on an auto liability claim, and $1,300,000 on a homeowners liability claim. Umbrella policies also typically provide coverage for claims that may be excluded by the primary policies such as false arrest, libel, slander, and nvasion of privacy.

Who needs it? The more assets you have, the more you would want to consider umbrella insurance because sadly, there are people in this world that take advantage of situations to file law suits. The best advice I ever received about protecting myself from law suits was this: *If you are in a car accident, never hand the other driver your business card*—especially if you are a doctor, lawyer, or business owner. You don't want to give them reason to think suing you would result in financial reward.

Part IV: Estate Planning

Estate planning is a process to make sure that what you own goes where you want, the way you want, if you become disabled or die. It is also where you designate guardians for minor children or dependent adults. Many people believe they don't have an "estate" and therefore don't need a plan, but what they don't realize is this plan is not only for what they currently own, but it also applies to what they may own or be entitled to in the future, like royalties, settlements, earnings or bonuses. You can't take your stuff with you when you die, but you can make things easier and clearer for those left behind, while also being smart about taxes and attorney's fees.

Elements of an Estate Plan:

Basic Estate Plan: Includes a Will, Power of Attorney, and Advanced Directive

Will—A set of instructions about the distribution of your assets and the guardianship of your children. Your will is overseen by the state (this is called probate), is public (it's available for anyone to request and view), and requires an attorney to administer after death. When creating a Will you designate an executor; the person who will administer your will according to your wishes.

Last Will and Testament of Zelda
- establishes guardianship
- covers basic issues only regarding death
- public
- probate (court)

Power of Attorney—A document that allows you to designate someone to manage your financial affairs if you are incapacitated or unavailable (out of the country, for example). You determine what they are able to do—like signing checks, making deposits, withdrawing money, making trades in a brokerage account, etc.

Advanced Directive for Healthcare and POLST—tools to help you think through and communicate your end-of-life choices.

- **Advanced Directive** – A written statement of your wishes, choices, and preferences regarding end-of-life care. This includes two documents:

    ~ *Living Will* – Describes your wishes and what you want or don't want for end-of-life care. For example, "If I'm unable to breathe on my own, then...."

    ~ *Durable Power of Attorney for Healthcare* – This document allows you to appoint someone to make medical decisions for you if you are unable to speak. It's more flexible than a Living Will because it allows your representative to take the situation into consideration when making decisions, therefore does not list individual situations. Also called DPOH, Medical Power of Attorney, or Healthcare Agent.

- **POLST (Physician Orders for Life-Sustaining Treatment)** – This is a form that states what kind of medical treatment a patient wants toward the end of their life. Printed on bright pink paper, and signed by both a doctor and patient, POLST helps give seriously ill patients more control over their end-of-life care and stays with the patient across care settings. This complements, but does not replace, an advanced directive. POLST is currently endorsed in CA, HI, ID, LA, MD, MT, NY, NC, OR, PA, TN, UT, WA, WV, WY.

Trusts

A trust is a legal agreement that allows a person (the trustee) to control certain assets that have been listed in the agreement. Trusts avoid probate, which can be expensive and time-consuming. To be legitimate, a trust must have four parts.

1. **Grantor or Trust Maker:** person who creates the trust and usually owns the assets that will be put in the trust.
2. **Assets or Property:** real estate, money, collectibles, royalties, etc.
3. **Trustee:** person who manages the trust and makes distributions from it.
4. **Beneficiaries:** people or organizations that benefit from the trust.

Types of Trusts

Revocable Living Trust: The most common trust, the Revocable Living Trust, is used for comprehensive estate planning. It provides greater flexibility and more specific directions than a will, as well as guidelines for managing the trust assets in the event of disability or death. The person who creates the trust typically retains control over it, and can change it while they are alive and mentally capable.

A Revocable Living Trust can change or be "revoked" through a trust amendment. At death, this trust becomes irrevocable. The grantor is often the trustee until either mentally incapacitated or dead. Within a trust document you will find a pour-over will (in the event an asset was not correctly titled in the name of the trust), a power-of-attorney, and an advanced directive for healthcare. There are many types of living trusts, all with strange names like: QTIP trust, A/B Trust, By Pass Trust, and so on.

Irrevocable Trust: An Irrevocable Trust cannot be changed once the grantor assigns her assets to it. Often an irrevocable trust is used to remove assets from a large estate to avoid estate taxes, and protect the assets from creditors and predators. Someone who is a "trust fund baby" most likely receives income from an irrevocable trust—they have to follow the distribution guidelines set up by their relative and can't change them. The beneficiary of an irrevocable trust may receive income or access to the principal according to how the original trust document was written. They do not control the asset and cannot change the way it was written without going to court.

ELEMENTS of a ROCKING ESTATE PLAN

WILL or TRUST $-$$$$$
With Power of Attorney, Advanced Health Care Directive

BENEFICIARY DESIGNATIONS NO COST-$
In alignment with overall plan—these supersede the will or trust, so be certain you have them the way you want.

REGISTRATION of all ACCOUNTS NO COST-$
In alignment with overall plan—this refers to the names on your accounts. Is your bank account in your name only, joint name, or the name of your trust? This is important; because if an account is in your name only, your partner won't have access to them if you are disabled—even if your partner is the designated beneficiary in your will, it could be months or years before your estate makes it through probate.

Consider (carefully!): joint ownership; creating a trust or using "transfer on death" (TOD) on your non-retirement accounts (this effectively gives a beneficiary designation to bank/brokerage accounts and avoids probate).

WRITTEN INSTRUCTIONS NO COST-$
About the distribution of personal property

FUNERAL PLANS/ARRANGEMENTS $-$$$
Detailed, purchased and communicated to family

WRITTEN GUIDELINES to CHILDREN NO COST-$
And/or guardians of children should you not be able to raise them—what are your wishes, values, priorities, and stipulations?

Part V: Terms You Should Know

Annual Gift Exemption—The amount you can give another person, annually, without having to file a gift tax return. Currently this is $14,000 (2013).

APR (Annual Percentage Rate)—The interest paid over a 12 month period.

Asset— A resource of monetary value including cash, accounts receivable, inventory, real estate, machinery, collectibles, and securities.

Asset Allocation—A way of balancing risk and reward through choosing how much you have invested in different types of assets (stocks, bonds, cash, real estate).

Capital Gain/Loss— The difference between the cost basis of an asset and its current market value. "Realized" capital gain means that you've actually sold the asset, and "unrealized" means that on paper you have a capital gain or loss. Short-term capital gain/loss is any gain or loss that has occured in less than 365 days; Long term is when the asset has been held for over one year.

Certificate of Deposit (CD)— An interest-bearing investment from a bank that has a rate of return (interest rate) and a date of maturity (how long you are committing your money). The interest rate depends on the amount of money and length of time of the deposit.

Charitable Deduction—What you can deduct from your income taxes each year for giving to charity. The deduction varies depending on your income and the type of donation (cash, in-kind donations, cars, etc.)

Charitable Giving in your Estate Plan—Designating part of your estate to go to charity either through beneficiary designations (life insurance, retirement plans, annuities) or in your will/trust.

Compound vs. Simple Interest— The difference between simple and compound interest is the difference between night and day. Remember this: Simple interest grows slowly, compounding speeds up the process. Simple interest is earning interest on your principal, and compound interest is earning interest on your principal plus interest- kind of like a snowball effect.

Cost Basis— What you paid for an asset (real estate, stock, business) plus adjustments. For example: A rental house—if you pay $100,000, and remodel the bathroom for $25,000. The cost basis is now $125,000. Likewise, if you buy $10,000 of stock (in a non-retirement account), and over the five years you've owned it, you received or reinvested $1,000 in dividends, then your cost basis is $11,000. Cost basis is used to calculate capital gain and loss for tax purposes.

Dollar Cost Averaging (DCA)— This is where you invest in stocks or mutual funds for a fixed amount every month or quarter. By buying over a period of time, you minimize the risk of buying at a bad time, and the price paid is averaged over time. Investing into a 401k every month is a form of dollar cost averaging.

Donor Advised Fund—An easy-to-establish, low cost, flexible vehicle for charitable giving this is an alternative to direct giving or creating a private foundation.

DOW Jones Industrial Average (DJIA)— An index made up of thirty of the largest and most widely held companies traded on the New York Stock Exchange. The DJIA is considered to represent the movement of the entire US stock market.

Equity— 1) What is left after subtracting what you owe from the value of your asset. The equity in your house = market value minus mortgage(s); 2) Something you have partial ownership of, such as a stock.

FDIC (Federal Deposit Insurance Corporation)—A US government corporation that guarantees the safety of savings accounts at member banks for up to $250,000.

FINRA (Financial Industry Regulatory Authority)—A private corporation that provides financial regulation of member brokerage firms and securities exchanges. This is the successor to the NASD.

HELOC (Home Equity Line of Credit)—A loan that is secured by the equity in your home.

High Yield or Junk Bonds— Bonds with low credit ratings. The investor who purchases high yield bonds typically is taking more risk in order to get a better yield on the bond. High Yield bonds are rated 'BB', 'B', 'CCC', etc.

Index— An imaginary portfolio of securities (stocks or bonds) representing a particular market or a portion of it. The Standard & Poor's 500 is one of the world's most popular indexes, and is commonly used as a benchmark for the US stock market. It contains the 500 largest US companies. Other prominent indexes include the MSCI EAFE (foreign stocks in Europe, Australasia, Far East) and the Lehman Brothers Aggregate Bond Index (total bond market). Each index is unique in its calculation methodology and so paying attention to the percentage change in the index is more important than the actual numeric value of it.

Indices are also used to gauge activity in an economy. The best-known economic index in the United States is the Consumer Price Index (CPI), which measures inflation.

Index Fund— Since you can't, technically, invest in an index, index mutual funds and exchange-traded funds (based on indexes) allow you to invest in securities representing broad market segments and/or the total market. An S&P 500 Index fund will have the same 500 stocks as the index. The only way a stock is added or subtracted from the fund is if a company is added/removed from the Index itself.

Initial Public Offering (IPO)— The first stock offering of a new, publically traded company.

Investment Grade Bonds—Bonds with a high credit rating and therefore are considered to have a low risk of default. Bond rating firms, such as Standard & Poor's, use upper- and lower-case letters 'A' and 'B' to identify a bond's credit quality rating. 'AAA' and 'AA' (high credit quality) and 'A' and 'BBB' (medium credit quality) are considered investment grade. Credit ratings for bonds below these designations ('BB', 'B', 'CCC', etc.) are considered low credit quality, and are commonly referred to as "junk bonds".

Liquidity— The ability or ease with which assets can be converted into cash; also the degree to which one can obtain the full cash value of an investment.

Money Market— A type of mutual fund that invests in short-term securities, such as Certificates of Deposits and Treasury Bills, that aim to always be valued at $1 per share. (Tends to have a higher yield than savings accounts, and is not FDIC insured.)

Margin Loan— A loan taken from a brokerage account using securities as collateral.

Net Worth— The value of what you own minus what you owe.

Assets – Liabilities (debt) = Net Worth

Portfolio— In art, this refers to a collection of your work, traditionally held in a binder. In the world of finance, your portfolio is made up your investments and cash—stocks, bonds, mutual funds, real estate (not your home), life insurance (with cash value), annuities, precious metals, collectibles, gas/mineral rights and business holdings.

Registration— The way an account is titled, such as Anne S. Rockstar, or The Rockstar Family Trust.

Retirement Plans (Employer- Sponsored):

401k—An employer sponsored plan that lets eligible employees to make contributions directly from their paycheck. These contributions are made on a pretax basis, and earnings grow on a tax-deferred basis. When assets are withdrawn from the plan in retirement they will be 100% taxable as ordinary income.

Roth 401k—Many plans now offer a Roth component to their 401ks. You can contribute some or all of your entire annual contribution limit to the Roth 401k side of the plan. These contributions are made on an after-tax basis, therefore when assets are withdrawn from the plan in retirement they will be 100% tax free.

403b— A US retirement plan offered through public organizations and non-profits. It has the same tax treatment as a 401k plan.

SEP—Simplified Employee Pension IRA- A retirement plan that a small business owner or solopreneur can establish. Contributions are tax deductible and are limited to a percent of total net profit. At retirement the funds will be 100% taxable when withdrawn.

SIMPLE IRA—(Savings Incentive Match Plan for Employees) A type of tax-deferred employer sponsored retirement plan used by small businesses. It is simpler and less costly to administer than 401k plans. Contribution limits for SIMPLE plans are lower than 401ks: $12,000, with $2,500 catch-up if over 50, as compared to $17,500 plus a $5,000 catch-up.

Retirement Plans (Individual):

Traditional IRA (Individual Retirement Account)—The IRA is held at a custodian institution such as a bank or brokerage, and may be invested in anything that the custodian allows (for instance, a bank may allow CDs and a brokerage may allow mutual funds). To qualify to take your contribution as a tax deduction you must meet eligibility requirements based on income, filing status, and availability of other retirement plans. An IRA is tax-deferred until assets are withdrawn, at which time they are taxed as ordinary income. Currently the maximum contribution is $5,500 with an additional $1,000 if you are over 50.

Roth IRA—The Roth allows you to contribute after-tax dollars, and is therefore not tax deductible. The advantage to this is that since taxes have been paid on the principal (amount contributed), the investment grows tax-deferred and after age 59½ you can withdrawal the funds and they are 100% tax-free.

Risk Tolerance— A measure of your ability to take risks with your investments (your comfort zone). Your tolerance is evaluated by trying to understand how you behave when market conditions change. Your tolerance for risk will change with age and life circumstances.

SEC (Securities and Exchange Commission)—Federal agency responsible for enforcing federal securities laws and regulating the securities industry and exchanges in the U.S.

Security— A financial tool that is either: ownership (as in a stock or mutual fund); loanership (as in a bond); or the right to ownership (as in an option).

SIPC (Securities Investors Protection Corporation)—a company that protects investors from financial harm if a broker-dealer fails.

Standard & Poor's (S&P)— The S&P 500 index measures the overall change in the value of 500 stocks of the largest firms in the US. It is used as a benchmark of market performance.

Tax Loss Harvesting— The process of selling securities in a portfolio to realize the losses with the intention of putting the proceeds back in the market. Often done by people with significant capital gains who want to minimize the taxes paid that year.

Yield— The value found by dividing the amount of interest paid on a bond, by the price, thus measuring the income from a bond. (The term also refers to the dividend from stock divided by its price. Yield, however, is not a measure of total return since it does not include capital gains or losses.)

YTD (Year to Date)—Used when describing performance on securities measured from Jan 1st to the current date.

Zelda's Financial Toolbox

Websites:

Investopedia.com

Women in Financial Education: wife.org

Daily Worth: dailyworth.com

Creative Wealth International (great programs for children)

Money Coaching Institute: moneycoachinginstitute.com

You Need a Budget.com

Money Books:

The Money Book for Freelancers, Part-Timers and the Self-Employed,
by Joseph d'Agnese & Denise Kiernan

The Accounting Game: Basic Accounting Fresh from the Lemonade Stand
by Darrell Mullis & Judith Orloff

Emotional Currency: A Woman's Guide to Building a Healthy Relationship with Money, by Kate Levinson Ph.D.

Financial Recovery: Developing a Healthy Relationship with Money,
by Karen McCall

Finding a Financial Planner:

www.cfp.net/find

www.letsmakeaplan.org

www.prideplanners.com

Resources for Finding Health Insurance:

eHealthInsurance.com,

einsurance.com

GoHealthinsurance.com

Insure.com

healthcare.gov

aarp.com (if you are over 50)

National Assoc. of Self Employed (www.nase.com)

*Y*ou feel smarter now, right? I sure hope so. I find a new gem every time I read this thing! That's what makes a field guide such an asset. You can reference it again and again no matter where you are in your adventure.

I hope this financial glossary has clarified some concepts, or helped to shape your questions, so you'll feel cool and collected when talking about money matters with your advisor/friends/partner/loved ones.

There is even more for you to enjoy at lunajaffe.com. Bring your friends, bring your creativity and bring your questions so I can answer them on my blog!

Imagine a world where creative, free-spirited, adventurous souls have their money act together! Loving, beautiful, creative powerhouses rocking the universe with our financial prowess and impact. Now that's what I'm talking about!

I hope to see you soon at lunajaffe.com where more resources and opportunities await you.

Wildly Yours,

Zelda and The Whole Wild Money Team

P.S. Keep in touch, yeah?
zelda@lunajaffe.com

About Luna Jaffe

Luna Jaffe is a seasoned Certified Financial Planner™, artist, writer and professional speaker who helps frustrated creatives and entrepreneurs develop money savvy so they can become financially confident.

A former professional artist and psychotherapist, and an entrepreneur for over 25 years, she deeply understands the challenges faced by creatives in managing and growing their money.

Luna says, "I wasn't born with a money gene, and most likely you weren't either. In my twenties, I was an artist, painting on silk and travelling the world. **Money was an afterthought.** Then I earned a Master's degree in depth psychology, merging my love of art and psyche, soul and spirit. **Money was moving to the front seat.** Working for a Fortune 100 company as a corporate trainer and coach awakened the possibility of consistent income. **Money was a vehicle for my dreams.** I gave birth at 40, experiencing the messy miracle of life. **Money mattered.** Then 911 happened, I got ill and was laid off...all with a toddler in my arms. **Money became critical.** I was not looking for financial planning, but apparently it was looking for me. I was recruited. I feared I couldn't learn about money, then dared myself to try. I was inspired, doggedly determined, unstoppable. **Money became a friend, mentor, companion and advocate."**

Over the past ten years Luna has developed an innovative financial planning process that elegantly combines creativity and psychology, right brain and left brain, body and soul. In 2010 she founded Lunaria Financial, Ltd, a boutique financial planning firm in Portland, Oregon. She holds a BA in Bilingual Education from UCSC and a MA in Depth Psychology from Pacifica Graduate Institute.

When she's not working with clients, speaking or teaching, she's either playing guitar, hanging out with her teenager and friends, dancing or digging in the garden.

Securities & Advisory Services Offered Through KMS Financial Services, Inc. Member FINRA/SIPC

INDEX

Standard & Poor's (S&P), 211, 212, 214

stockholders, 166, 167, 168

stocks, 166, 167, 168, 170, 172
    aggressive growth, 171, 172
    capitalization and, 174, 177, 181
    diversification of, 174-76, 177
    dividends and, 166, 168, 170, 171, 214
    domestic, 175, 177
    exchange-traded funds (ETFs) and, 185
    global, 175, 177
    growth, 171, 172
    growth and income, 171, 172
    international, 175, 177
    mutual funds and, 178, 181, 184
    risk and, 171, 172, 174-76
    socially responsible investing (SRI) and, 191, 192
    taxation and, 194, 196, 197

sustainable investing. See socially responsible investing (SRI)

taxable accounts, 194, 195, 196, 197

taxation, 194-97. See also under annuities; bank accounts; bonds; cash; 401k; interest; investment accounts; IRA; life insurance; mutual funds; retirement; Roth 401k; stocks; trusts

tax deferred accounts, 194, 195, 196, 197

tax deferred and tax free accounts, 194, 195-97

tax deferred annuities, 189, 190, 196

taxes. See taxation

tax free bonds, 170

tax free exchanges, 190

tax loss harvesting, 214

term life insurance, 199-200, 201

traditional IRA, 194, 195, 196, 197, 213

transfer on death (TOD), 209

trustee, 207

trusts, 195, 207-8, 209
    beneficiaries of, 207, 208, 209
    irrevocable, 208
    living, 208
    revocable living, 208
    taxation and, 195, 208

umbrella insurance, 205

universal life (UL) insurance, 200-201

values. See socially responsible investing (SRI)

variable annuities, 189

variable universal life insurance, 200

websites, 215

whole life insurance, 200-201

wills, 206, 207, 208, 209
    beneficiaries of, 209

yield, 167, 168, 170, 214. See also high yield bonds

YTD (year to date), 214

Join the Wild Money Revolution!

☼ Join the Wild Money Tribe, come to a retreat or take the Wild Money course online

More information at www.lunajaffe.com

☼ Hire Luna to speak or teach at your events!
Call 503-452-7000 or info@lunajaffe.com

☼ Sign-up for the Call of the Wild

Call of the Wild
A free monthly Q & A
call for creatives who need
to talk about their
relationship with money

☼ Share your images, writing, questions and experiences with the community: info@lunajaffe.com

☼ Best of all—Send Snail Mail!

I'd love to hear from you! Real mail is such a treat!

Luna Jaffe
7837 SW Capitol Highway, Suite C
Portland, Oregon 97219

Visit www.lunajaffe.com to purchase your copy of

WILD MONEY:
A CREATIVE JOURNEY TO FINANCIAL WISDOM